Also by Perla Meyers

The Peasant Kitchen

*Perla Meyers' From Market to
    Kitchen Cookbook*

The Seasonal Kitchen

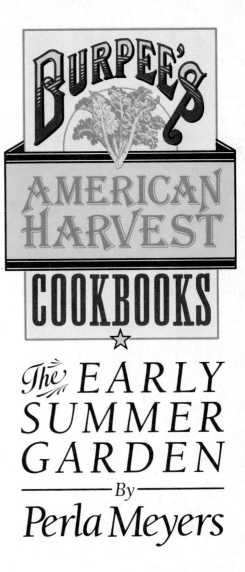

BURPEE'S

AMERICAN HARVEST

COOKBOOKS

The EARLY
SUMMER
GARDEN
— By —
Perla Meyers

A FIRESIDE BOOK
Published by Simon & Schuster Inc.
New York London Toronto Sydney Tokyo

. . . .

To Michael diBeneditto for his strong, never failing support, for his help and dedication, and for his spirited thoroughness in testing the recipes.

. . . .

Photography by Simon Metz
Food Styling by Michael diBeneditto

A FIRESIDE BOOK, published by Simon & Schuster Inc., Simon & Schuster Building, Rockefeller Center, 1230 Avenue of the Americas, New York, NY 10020.

FIRESIDE and colophon are registered trademarks of Simon & Schuster Inc.

DESIGNED BY JOEL AVIROM

Manufactured in the United States of America

10 9 8 7 6 5 4 3 2 1

Library of Congress Cataloging-in-Publication Data

Meyers, Perla.
    The early summer garden/by Perla Meyers; photography by Simon Metz; food styling by Michael di-Beneditto.
    p.   cm.—(Burpee's American harvest cookbooks)
    "A Fireside book."
    Includes index.
    ISBN 0-671-63363-5 (pbk.): $8.95
    1. Cookery (Vegetables)   2. Vegetable gardening.
I. W. Atlee Burpee Company.   II. Title.   III. Series:
Meyers, Perla. Burpee's American harvest cookbooks.
TX801.M49 1988
641.6'5—dc 19   87-28545
                                                 CIP

I wish to thank Dean & DeLuca, Wolfman Gold, and The Silo for the use of their accessories.

Picture Credits: Burpee—7, 12, 17, 19, 22, 24, 28, 29, 34, 36, 38, 45, 50, 53, 54, 56, 59, 62, 64, 66, 69, 71, 73, 75, 78, 80, 83, 88, 89, 99, 100, 103, 104, 109, 117; Bettmann Archive—8, 85, 92, 126; Dover Publications *Food and Drink*—5, 26, 27, 29, 38, 43, 61, 67, 106, 110, 113, 121; Dover Publications *Goods and Merchandise*—70, 91. Every effort has been made to locate and credit other artwork used in this book. If any has been overlooked, we welcome credit information which will be included in future editions.

C · O · N · T · E · N · T · S

Introduction 6

SNAP BEANS 8

CARROTS 22

CORN 34

CUCUMBERS 48

PEPPERS 62

SWISS CHARD 78

TOMATOES 86

ZUCCHINI (Summer Squash) 104

Index 122

Growing Chart 124

From the time I was a small child watching over a simple garden of radishes, lettuces, and carrots, I have been in awe of the vigor and promise of each fragile seedling that pokes through the earth. When I finally grew up and had a place to start a garden of my own, I naturally sent away for my first Burpee catalog. It was a great inspiration and turned gardening into a new experience for me.

Now, come February and the latest Burpee catalog in hand, the dead of winter is far from my mind; I fill my thoughts with the coming season. This is a time when I can leisurely explore the impressive varieties of "garden classics" as well as the new and uncommon vegetables that will yield optimum flavor, variety, and the longest possible harvest. Fresh vegetables never disappoint. Perhaps that is why they play an essential part in every major cuisine. For me no meal is complete without a vegetable, whether in the main course, a soup, or a salad.

As a cook and a gardener I find the vegetable garden inspires lightly sauced pastas, vegetable-studded pizzas, deeply flavored soups, and inventive casseroles. And I know that whatever my choices, Burpee seeds will produce wonderful vegetables. That has been the Burpee guarantee for more than 100 years.

The company was founded in 1876 by W. Atlee Burpee, an 18-year-old poultry breeder whose small catalog of poultry and livestock included seeds imported from Europe. Seed sales soon dominated the business. In 1888 Burpee set up his own seed-testing station in Doylestown, Pennsylvania, and by the end of the century had one of the world's largest mail-order seed houses. Burpee is still dominant, but its impact has been even greater than its position in the seed business, for whether one gardens or not, every American has enjoyed the benefits of Burpee's unique vegetable developments. Such varieties as Fordhook bush lima beans and Golden Bantam corn are benchmarks in the history of American agriculture and standard items in the national diet. The founder's son, David Burpee, took over the company and over the years introduced the world's first hybrid tomatoes, cucumbers, and other vegetables. Burpee's Big Boy hybrid tomato, introduced in 1949, is still one of America's most popular.

Burpee seeds today are planted in millions of American gardens. The company is constantly keeping pace with our changing lifestyles, the increasing interest in home gardening, and the endless American appetite for new products. Faster maturing plants with greater resistance to disease are being bred, as well as those with shorter vines, to fit and thrive in our small suburban—and urban—gardens. Such stylish greens as arugula and radicchio, until recently encountered only in fashionable restaurants, are now available to the home gardener.

For me, the garden is a natural extension of the kitchen, and Burpee's new or improved varieties only serve to enlarge the possibilities. Along with the increased awareness in this country of all things fresh is the great inspiration of many American cooks and chefs who now have so many varieties of vegetables and herbs available to them. This cookbook series takes advantage of those current trends. The Burpee American Harvest Cookbooks are collections of carefully created recipes that look first of all to the best produce available—that which is grown and harvested by the home gardener at the peak of freshness, flavor, and goodness. These are not vegetarian cookbooks but books that look to excellent produce as the center of a dish and a meal; by their very nature they also help us celebrate seasons at the table.

Here in *The Early Summer Garden* are recipes based on that most extravagant growing season. Tomatoes, the favorite crop of the home gardener, appear here along with the other stars of the season, such as cucumbers, peppers, and zucchini, and the one that perhaps defines American summer eating more than any other, corn. Here, they are in appetizers, soups, tarts, main dishes, and inventive salads that are simple and quick. I hope that they please you as much as creating them has pleased me.

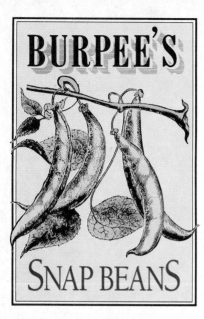

BURPEE'S

SNAP BEANS

Although snap beans are available almost year-round at supermarkets, what's missing from the grocer's vegetable is the audible "snap" of the pods that indicates good crunchy eating. For that, you really must rely on fresh-picked beans from the garden.

Many people still refer to snap beans as "string" beans. But the old name no longer applies because most modern varieties are stringless. The pods of old-fashioned types were joined down the back by tough fibers, or strings that had to be removed before the pods could be cooked. Preparing today's varieties requires nothing more than snapping off the stem-end tips.

What endears snap beans to a cook is versatility—perfect with every kind of meat, poultry, and fish, they also make terrific salad ingredients. One of my favorite bean salads is the classic *salade Niçoise,* from the south of France, which combines cooked cooled pods marinated in a mustard vinaigrette and tossed with slices of tiny new potatoes, flaked tuna, olives, and a handful of basil leaves. For an elegant first course to a summer dinner, try a salad of snap beans and diced shrimp dressed with walnut oil and sherry vinegar. Or revitalize leftover beans with a sprinkling of olive oil and lemon juice and then combine them with some mixed salad greens fresh from the garden.

Probably the simplest and most popular way to serve snap beans is steamed and buttered. However, I prefer a different basic preparation that offers greater possibilities. I cook snap beans in plenty of lightly salted boiling water for three to five minutes, depending on the size and maturity of the pods. (Ideally, cooked beans should soften yet retain some crunchiness—taste one to judge readiness.) As soon as they are done, drain and run under cold water. This stops any further cooking and lets the beans hold their bright green color. To bring out the very best flavor, I melt three tablespoons of butter in a large nonstick skillet and then gently toss the beans for only a minute or two. Do not sauté beans; this causes them to lose color and taste. Once the beans are buttered, you can add a variety of fresh herbs, such as dill or chives, or a touch of heavy cream plus two to three spoonfuls of

sour cream and a sprinkling of grated Parmesan. Snap beans should always be cooked whole. Even for a recipe that calls for cut beans, it is best to do so after pods have been blanched.

Some cookbooks call for French-style beans, in which the pods are cut into halves or quarters lengthwise and perhaps cross-wise as well before cooking. Not only is this technique time con-suming, but it produces a water-soaked bean that is neither tasty nor attractive. If you pick your beans when young and slender, they will be close in texture and appearance to the true French string bean, a type not often available in the United States.

S·T·O·R·A·G·E

Beans keep well refrigerated in a plastic bag up to a week. Shell beans and lima beans should be kept in their pods until just before cooking.

Beans freeze well; freezing changes their texture but they do preserve a good taste. To freeze, blanch the beans for two min-utes, then run under cold water to stop further cooking. Cool completely and freeze in freezer bags.

G·A·R·D·E·N·I·N·G

Some snap bean plants are bushy, while others form vigorous vines that attach themselves to poles or other supports. "Bush" beans, which are usually planted in rows, rarely grow taller than two feet. Because they mature in under sixty days, you can have several harvests throughout summer by making successive plant-ings from mid-spring to early summer. "Pole" beans take longer to mature than bush varieties but are far more prolific, producing pods for six to eight weeks. For a small garden I find pole varieties the better choice. Whether trained onto rough-hewn poles (six to eight feet high), wooden tripods, ready-made "bean towers," fences, or garden netting, plants take up air space rather than valuable ground space.

Bean seedlings do not transplant well, so it is best to sow seeds directly in place. But wait until soil has warmed and frost is no longer a danger. Otherwise, seeds may fail to germinate. Wherever beans are grown for the first time, it is a good idea to add nitrogen-fixing bacteria to the soil. These microbes, which are available commercially, enable beans and other legumes to absorb needed nitrogen from the atmosphere. Bigger and better harvests generally result.

Whatever supports you choose for your pole beans should be set in place before seeds are sown. Ten-foot poles should be sunk at least two feet into the earth at two- to three-foot intervals. Trellises should be anchored to the ground to prevent toppling in high wind. At planting time I like to apply some Burpee fertilizer to get vines off to a quick start. It may be necessary to guide young vines to their supports. I usually wind the plants counterclockwise—the direction they grow naturally—around the bases of the poles.

Dry soil in mid-season may cause developing pods to shrivel, and yanking nearby weeds can easily damage a bean plant's shallow root system. Applying mulch is the best solution to both problems. A four-inch layer of salt hay or other mulch material will retain soil moisture while smothering weeds.

There is an embarrassment of snap bean riches to choose from. Among the bush beans, I prefer a variety known as Greensleeves, a disease-resistant plant that sports exceptionally dark green pods. This variety and Tenderpod are extra-tender, require less time in cooking or blanching, and are the varieties of choice for serving raw on relish trays. As a contrast I sometimes grow Burpee's Brittle Wax with lemon yellow pods and a milder, sweeter taste than green beans. An outstanding pole variety is Kentucky Wonder; the green pods are up to nine inches long. For purees, in stews, in a gutsy tomato sauce for braising, I like Romano, whose flat pods have a wonderfully meaty texture. Another interesting and relatively new bean is Royal Burgundy. The pods have a beautiful dark purple color which turns green when cooked.

PICKLED GREEN AND YELLOW BEANS

Pack raw green and yellow snap beans in 4 hot, pint jars vertically. Place 1 unpeeled garlic clove, 1 chili pepper, and 1 head dill in each jar. Combine ⅓ cup sugar, ¼ cup coarse salt, 2½ cups water, 2½ cups cider vinegar, and 2 tablespoons pickling spices in saucepan. Bring to a boil and simmer 15 minutes. Pour over beans, cover, and process 15 minutes in boiling water bath. Cool and store 3 months before serving. Makes 4 pints.

Pick bush beans after they are firm enough to snap when bent but before the seeds inside become visibly enlarged. Bean plants are brittle, so harvest with a gentle touch. I hold a pod's stem in one hand while plucking off the pod with the other. It is essential to remove any older or undesirable pods if individual plants are to remain productive for a full two to three weeks. Remember to be conscientious about harvesting. The more beans you pick, the more you get.

R · E · C · I · P · E · S

Green Bean & Radish Salad in Sour Cream Vinaigrette 13

Bean Salad Niçoise 14

Warm Green Bean Salad with Crisp Potato Circles 15

Green & Wax Bean Salad with a Mayonnaise Vinaigrette 16

Sauté of Two Beans with Tomatoes, Onions & Tuna 17

Viennese Green Beans in Piquant Tomato Sauce 18

Puree of Green Beans with Sour Cream & Parmesan 19

A Soup of Mixed Beans alla Milanese (with Basil & Pastina) 20

Green Bean & Pasta Salad with Basil Dressing 21

Green Bean & Radish Salad in Sour Cream Vinaigrette

1. Bring plenty of lightly salted water to a boil, add the beans, and cook until just tender, about 6–7 minutes. Drain and immediately run under cold water to stop further cooking.

2. Transfer the beans to a serving bowl, sprinkle with 1 tablespoon vinegar and 2 tablespoons oil, toss, and set aside.

3. In a small bowl combine the remaining vinegar, sour cream, and oil. Whisk the dressing until smooth. Season with salt and pepper.

4. Add the radishes, scallions, and dressing to the beans and toss the salad gently with two spoons. Let the salad marinate at room temperature for 2 hours before serving.

5. Serve slightly chilled accompanied by French bread.

V·A·R·I·A·T·I·O·N

I often turn this refreshing salad into a hearty luncheon or supper dish by adding a cup of smoked turkey cut into fine julienne strips or a combination of a julienne of Gruyère cheese and smoked ham.

1 pound green beans, trimmed
3 tablespoons red wine vinegar
6 tablespoons olive oil
4 tablespoons sour cream
Coarse salt and freshly ground black pepper
2 cups finely sliced radishes (a combination of both red and white)
½ cup finely minced scallions

SERVES 6

HOMEMADE MAYONNAISE

In a blender combine 1 whole egg, 1 egg yolk, 2–3 teaspoons lemon juice or vinegar, and salt and white pepper to taste. With blender at top speed, add ¾ cup vegetable oil by droplets until mixture begins to thicken. Add remaining oil in a steady stream until incorporated. Keep in refrigerator in tightly covered jar. Makes 1¼ cups.

Bean Salad Niçoise

1 pound green beans, trimmed

1 small red onion, peeled and thinly
   sliced

⅔–1 cup Basil Vinaigrette
   (see below)

12 ripe cherry tomatoes, cut in half

1 can (6½ ounces) light tuna,
   drained and flaked

18 small black oil-cured olives,
   preferably Niçoise

GARNISH

Strips of sweet red bell pepper or
   pimientos

2 hard-boiled eggs, peeled and
   quartered

SERVES 4–6

P·R·E·P·A·R·A·T·I·O·N

1. Bring plenty of lightly salted water to a boil in a large sauce-pan. Add green beans and cook for 6–7 minutes or until just tender. Drain and run under cold water to stop further cooking. Dry the green beans thoroughly on paper towels and set aside.

2. Transfer the beans to a large serving bowl together with the red onion and toss with ⅔ cup vinaigrette. Marinate at room temperature for 30 minutes.

3. Just before serving, add the cherry tomatoes, tuna, and olives. Taste and correct the seasoning. Add the remaining vinaigrette if desired. Serve at room temperature garnished with strips of red pepper or pimientos and quartered hard-boiled eggs.

R·E·M·A·R·K·S

Salad may also be served individually. In that case, place 1–2 leaves of Boston lettuce under each portion on individual salad plates.

PROVENÇALE VINAIGRETTE

In a small jar combine 1 tablespoon olive oil, 2–3 tablespoons red wine vinegar, 2 teaspoons Dijon mustard and 1 clove garlic, crushed. Season with salt and pepper. Cover and shake until smooth.

VARIATIONS:

Basic: Omit garlic
Herb: Add 2 tablespoons minced
   chives, parsley or dill
Basil: Eliminate the mustard and
   garlic. Add 2 tablespoons Basil
   Paste (page 20) and 2
   tablespoons finely minced
   shallots.

Warm Green Bean Salad with Crisp Potato Circles

P·R·E·P·A·R·A·T·I·O·N

1. Bring about 1 inch of lightly salted water to a boil in a large saucepan. Insert a vegetable steamer and top with the green beans. Cover and steam for about 8 minutes or until the beans are tender. Run the beans under cold water to stop further cooking, drain, and pat dry on paper towels. Set aside.

2. Preheat oven to 425° F.

3. Brush each of 2 cookie sheets with 3 teaspoons melted butter.

4. Arrange a single layer of potato slices in a slightly overlapping pattern to form three 5-inch circles on each cookie sheet. (You should use about 9–10 potato slices for each circle.) Season with salt and pepper.

5. Place the sheets one at a time in the center of the preheated oven and bake each for 12–15 minutes or until potatoes are nicely browned and crisp.

6. While the potatoes are baking, prepare the warm salad. In a heavy 10-inch skillet sauté the diced bacon over medium heat until lightly browned. Remove with a slotted spoon and reserve.

7. Discard all but 3 tablespoons fat from the skillet and add the olive oil. When hot, add the shiitake or cultivated mushrooms and sliced garlic. Toss in the hot fat for 30 seconds. Add the green beans and reserved bacon and season with salt and pepper. Toss for another 30 seconds or until just heated through. Remove the skillet from the heat, let cool slightly, and add the vinegar. Taste and correct the seasoning.

8. To serve, divide the warm green bean salad among 6 individual serving plates. Top each with a crisp potato circle and serve at once.

1 pound green beans, trimmed
Salt
6 teaspoons unsalted butter, melted
1 all-purpose potato (about 8 ounces), peeled and very thinly sliced
Freshly ground black pepper
¼ pound lean bacon, cut into ¼-inch dice
4–5 tablespoons olive oil, preferably extra-virgin
8 fresh shiitake mushrooms or regular cultivated mushrooms, stemmed and caps thinly sliced
2 medium cloves garlic, peeled and thinly sliced
2–3 tablespoons red wine vinegar, preferably sherry

SERVES 6

Green & Wax Bean Salad with a Mayonnaise Vinaigrette

Begin this recipe 24 hours or so before you plan to serve.

6 small red potatoes (about 1 pound), unpeeled

½ pound green beans and ½ pound yellow wax beans

2 medium carrots, peeled and thinly sliced

7–8 tablespoons Basic Vinaigrette (page 14)

2 tablespoons finely minced parsley

2 medium scallions, trimmed and finely minced

Salt and freshly ground black pepper

2 tablespoons Homemade Mayonnaise (page 13)

GARNISH

2–3 tablespoons finely minced fresh parsley

Sieved hard-boiled eggs

SERVES 4–6

P·R·E·P·A·R·A·T·I·O·N

1. Bring plenty of lightly salted water to a boil in a large saucepan. Add the red potatoes and cook for 15–20 minutes or until tender. Do not overcook. Remove with a slotted spoon and set aside to cool.

2. Bring the water back to a boil, add the green and wax beans, and cook for 6–7 minutes or until just tender. Remove with a slotted spoon to a colander and run under cold water to stop further cooking. Trim and reserve.

3. Again bring water to a boil, add the carrot slices, and cook for 2–3 minutes or until just tender. Drain and run under water to stop further cooking.

4. Peel the potatoes and cut crosswise into ¼-inch slices. Transfer to a large serving bowl together with the green and wax beans and carrot slices. Add 4–5 tablespoons vinaigrette, parsley, and scallions and season with salt and a good grinding of black pepper. Toss gently so as not to break the potato slices. Cover and marinate at room temperature for 1 hour.

5. In a small mixing bowl whisk together the mayonnaise and remaining vinaigrette. Pour over the salad and toss gently. Taste and correct the seasoning. Cover and refrigerate overnight.

6. The next day remove the salad from the refrigerator 30 minutes before serving. Serve at room temperature, sprinkled with parsley and sieved hard-boiled eggs.

Sauté of Two Beans with Tomatoes, Onions & Tuna

P·R·E·P·A·R·A·T·I·O·N

1. In a large heavy skillet heat the olive oil over medium heat. Add the onion and garlic and cook until soft but not browned.

2. Add the tomatoes to the skillet, season with salt and pepper, and cook until all the tomato juices have evaporated, stirring gently. The tomatoes should still retain their shape.

3. Add the green beans, wax beans, olives, and tuna. Cover and cook until just heated through. Add the julienne of basil and taste and correct the seasoning. Serve warm.

V·A·R·I·A·T·I·O·N

You may also serve the beans at room temperature. Drizzle with 2–3 tablespoons olive oil and sprinkle with tiny capers, drained. Serve as part of a light luncheon.

3 tablespoons olive oil, preferably extra-virgin

1 large onion, peeled, quartered, and thinly sliced

1 large clove garlic, peeled and finely minced

6 ripe plum tomatoes, peeled and quartered

Salt and freshly ground black pepper

½ pound green beans and ½ pound yellow wax beans, trimmed and cooked

16 small black oil-cured olives, preferably Niçoise, pitted

1 can (6½ ounces) light tuna, drained and flaked

¼ cup fine julienne of fresh basil

SERVES 4–6

Viennese Green Beans in Piquant Tomato Sauce

1 pound green beans, trimmed

Salt

2 tablespoons unsalted butter

1 teaspoon olive oil

1 large red onion, peeled and finely
   minced

1 small dry cayenne pepper finely
   sliced or 1 small fresh

2 medium cloves garlic, peeled and
   finely minced

1½ teaspoons paprika, preferably
   imported

6–8 large ripe tomatoes, peeled,
   seeded, and chopped

Freshly ground black pepper

½ cup sour cream

Optional: 1 Beurre Manié
   (page 54)

SERVES 4–5

P·R·E·P·A·R·A·T·I·O·N

1. Bring lightly salted water to a boil. Add the beans and cook for 5 minutes or until crisp tender. Drain the beans and when cool enough to handle cut into 1-inch pieces. Set aside.

2. In a deep heavy skillet heat the butter and oil over low heat. Add the onion, cayenne pepper, and garlic and cook the mixture for 5–10 minutes without browning. Add the paprika and tomatoes. Bring to a boil, reduce heat, and simmer until all the tomato water has evaporated and the sauce is thick.

3. Add the beans, season with salt and pepper, and simmer for another 10 minutes. Add the sour cream and if the tomato sauce seems too thin, whisk in bits of the beurre manié and continue to simmer until the sauce is thick. Taste and correct the seasoning. Serve the beans hot as an accompaniment to chicken, veal, or pork dishes.

R·E·M·A·R·K·S

The entire dish can be made well ahead of time and reheated. I often use a mixture of both wax and green beans and add a small diced green bell pepper to the onion base for a change of flavor.

Puree of Green Beans with Sour Cream & Parmesan

P·R·E·P·A·R·A·T·I·O·N

1. Bring plenty of lightly salted water to a boil in a large saucepan. Add the green beans and cook until very tender, about 10 minutes. Drain well.

2. Combine the green beans, butter, sour cream, and dill in a food processor or blender. Season with salt and pepper and puree until smooth. Set aside.

3. Heat the oil in a medium skillet. Add the flour and cook, stirring constantly, until the mixture turns a hazelnut brown.

4. Immediately add the green bean puree and cook until just heated through. Add the Parmesan cheese and correct the seasoning. Serve hot.

1½ pounds green beans, trimmed
5 tablespoons unsalted butter
¼ cup sour cream
3–4 tablespoons finely minced fresh dill
Salt and freshly ground black pepper
3 tablespoons vegetable oil
2 tablespoons all-purpose flour
3 tablespoons freshly grated Parmesan cheese

SERVES 6–8

A Soup of Mixed Beans alla Milanese (with Basil & Pastina)

1 tablespoon unsalted butter

2 tablespoons olive oil, preferably extra-virgin

1 medium onion, peeled and finely minced

1 cup diced green beans and 1 cup diced yellow wax beans (about ½-inch pieces)

Salt and freshly ground black pepper

6 cups Chicken Stock (page 37) or bouillon

½ cup tiny pasta (tubettini, bows, or pastina)

3 tablespoons Basil Paste (see below)

GARNISH

1 cup freshly grated Parmesan cheese

SERVES 4–6

P·R·E·P·A·R·A·T·I·O·N

1. In a large heavy saucepan heat the butter and oil over medium heat. Add the onion, green and wax beans, and season with salt and pepper. Cover, reduce heat, and cook for 15 minutes, stirring often.

2. Add the stock and bring to a boil. Reduce heat and simmer for 15 minutes.

3. While the soup is simmering, bring salted water to a boil in a medium saucepan. Add the pasta and cook for 7–8 minutes or until barely tender. Do not overcook. Add 1 cup cold water to the pot to stop further cooking.

4. Drain the pasta and add it to the soup together with the basil paste. Cook the soup for another 2 minutes. Taste and correct the seasoning, adding a large grinding of black pepper.

5. Serve the soup in individual bowls with a side dish of freshly grated Parmesan cheese.

V·A·R·I·A·T·I·O·N

You may also add 1 cup finely shredded cooked chicken to the soup when adding the cooked pasta and basil paste.

BASIL PASTE

Place 4 cups tightly packed fresh basil leaves, stemmed, in food processor or blender. Puree with enough olive oil to make a smooth paste. Spoon into jars, add more oil to cover the surface, and cover tightly. Will keep in refrigerator for 1 week or frozen up to 3 months. Makes ½ cup.

Green Bean & Pasta Salad with Basil Dressing

1. Bring plenty of lightly salted water to a boil with the olive oil. Add the pasta and cook for 8–10 minutes or until just tender. Immediately add 2 cups cold water to stop further cooking. Drain well and transfer to a large serving bowl.

2. Toss the warm pasta with the basil vinaigrette, season with salt and pepper, and set aside to cool.

3. Add the red onions, zucchini, red peppers, green beans, tuna, olives, and cherry tomatoes and toss the salad gently. Cover and refrigerate overnight.

4. Remove the salad from the refrigerator 30 minutes before serving. Taste, correct the seasoning, and serve at room temperature.

2 tablespoons olive oil

½ pound fusilli, rotelle, or twists

10 tablespoons Basil Vinaigrette (page 14)

Salt and freshly ground black pepper

1 medium red onion, peeled and finely minced

2 small zucchini, trimmed and thinly sliced

2 red bell peppers, roasted, peeled, and thinly sliced (page 65)

½ pound green beans, cooked and cut into 2-inch pieces

1 can (6½ ounces) light tuna, drained and flaked

18 small black oil-cured olives, preferably Niçoise

12 ripe cherry tomatoes, cut in half

SERVES 6

BURPEE'S

CARROTS

Helping my father plant vegetables remains among my dearest childhood memories. I always waited with great anticipation for the first signs of seedlings, and of carrots, in particular, with their distinctive feathery tops. I could never resist pulling up just one to nibble, the tiny beginnings of a sweet, orange root. While tending my garden today, it is no less a pleasure to munch on freshly plucked baby carrots no bigger than a finger.

Carrots are among the most good-natured of vegetables; nearly effortless to grow, they can be picked when quite young or fully mature and are adaptable to an endless variety of preparations. Raw, this vegetable is far more versatile than usually given credit for, especially for quick summer snacks. One of my long-time favorites is raw, grated carrots sprinkled with some sugar and lemon juice. Our refrigerator always seemed stocked with a dish of this zesty slaw, sometimes enhanced with grated apples, raisins and diced walnuts. Raw, finely sliced carrots add a welcome crunch to a pasta salad or when marinated with cauliflower florets and finely sliced broccoli stalks in a mustard dressing. The flavors of carrots and broccoli in combination blend to produce a refreshing complement to roast meats, grilled fish and sautéed or barbecued chicken; despite their differences.

Carrots are essential in stocks and most vegetable soups as well as in many stews and sauces. Steamed or cooked whole, carrots work beautifully as an accompaniment to all meats, fish and poultry dishes. This is especially so if the roots are young; that is, picked prior to maturity. I usually cook them in a covered, 10-inch skillet with salted water, plus a large dollop of butter. When the carrots are tender, I drain off all but one-quarter cup of water, add a generous sprinkling of sugar and then let the carrots sit and absorb the pan juices. All buttery and sweetly glazed, the results glitter.

Braising is another excellent way to cook this vegetable, and one which I prefer when in need of a dish that can be prepared well in advance and reheated. The French method of braising

carrots is by far the most successful, cut into one-inch match-sticks and then lightly sautéed in butter with diced bacon cubes, a few garlic cloves and chicken broth to cover. When done, the carrots have a wonderful mellow flavor quite unlike any other preparation. The finished dish can be varied by adding a touch of cream, a few tiny white onions or cooked peas during reheating.

Whether eaten raw or to be cooked, young garden carrots must first be peeled lightly with a swivel blade peeler or scraped with a small sharp knife. After a good rinsing, they can be sliced, cubed, diced or cut into fine julienne strips. Baby carrots need only to be scrubbed with a stiff brush before they are briefly cooked or steamed—and nothing more. With these little jewels of summer, I find the simpler the preparation the better.

S · T · O · R · A · G · E

When buying carrots look for bright orange bunches with crisp, green, feathery tops. The carrots should be firm and well shaped. Avoid shriveled carrots with wilted tops.

To store, always remove the green tops and refrigerate the unwashed carrots in a plastic bag. They will keep for two to three weeks. Even after this time, carrots can still be used for stocks and in stews.

A surplus of garden fresh carrots can be frozen successfully, although, as with many vegetables, freezing changes their texture. I usually keep the baby carrots whole but scrape and then slice the large carrots into one-quarter-inch slices. Once they have been blanched for two to three mintues, I run them under cold water to cool and then pack them in plastic bags. Frozen carrots will keep for six to eight months.

G · A · R · D · E · N · I · N · G

Your soil will help determine the best type of carrots to grow. All carrots flourish in light, sandy, stoneless loam that can be worked to a depth of ten inches or more. No other soil will do for the long and elegantly tapered varieties such as Gold Pak. I am limited to growing shorter, stubbier varieties because my garden soil is heavy. Among the best baby carrots are Little Finger and Short 'n Sweet. These varieties manage in almost any soil, including planters and pots. Clay soils will certainly be improved by digging in organic matter before planting. But be careful about using manures. Unless well-rotted, they will cause carrots to become tough or malformed. For a continuous supply of carrots throughout summer, sow successive crops at three-week intervals starting in early spring. It's a good idea to cover newly sown rows with a thin layer of dried grass clippings to prevent the soil from forming a crust. Otherwise, tiny carrot sprouts may have trouble pushing through to daylight. The seeds germinate slowly, and soil should be kept quite moist until sprouts appear.

H · A · R · V · E · S · T · I · N · G

Harvesting can begin before the full sixty-five to eighty-five days it takes for most carrots to reach full size. Be sure to pick those plants with the biggest tops first. Some people do the reverse, hoping that all remaining carrots will grow as large as possible. With carrots, as with most vegetables, bigger is not better. To the contrary, the smaller the sweeter.

R · E · C · I · P · E · S	
Glazed Carrots with Brown Sugar & Mint	26
Carrot Soup with Fragrant Indian Spices	27
Carrot Clafoutis	28
Puree of Carrots with Crème Fraîche & Honey	29
Roast Pork with Carrots & Prunes in Sweet Port Wine Sauce	30
Creamy Carrot & Cabbage Slaw	31
Rice Pilaf of Carrots & Golden Raisins	32
Grated Carrot & Pineapple Muffins	33

Glazed Carrots with Brown Sugar & Mint

4 tablespoons unsalted butter

2 pounds medium carrots (about 12–14), trimmed, peeled, and cut into pieces ½ by ½ by 1 inch

Salt and freshly ground white pepper

1 teaspoon granulated sugar

½ cup water

2 tablespoons dark brown sugar

½ cup heavy cream

Pinch freshly grated nutmeg

2 tablespoons tiny fresh mint leaves

SERVES 6

P · R · E · P · A · R · A · T · I · O · N

1. Melt the butter in a large heavy skillet over medium heat. Add the carrots and season with salt, pepper, and sugar. Toss in the butter to glaze (about 3–4 minutes). Reduce the heat, add the water, cover, and simmer until tender (about 10–12 minutes).

2. Remove the cover, raise the heat, and cook until all the water has evaporated.

3. Add the brown sugar to the skillet and cook until melted. Add the heavy cream, bring to a boil, and reduce until the cream thickens and coats the carrots. Taste and correct the seasoning, adding a pinch of nutmeg and the mint leaves. Serve hot as an accompaniment to roast or grilled meats.

Carrot Soup with Fragrant Indian Spices

P·R·E·P·A·R·A·T·I·O·N

1. In a large heavy casserole, heat the butter, add the onion, and cook over low heat until soft but not brown. Add the brown sugar and spices and cook the mixture for 1 minute longer.

2. Add the carrots, potatoes, and stock, bring to a boil, reduce heat. Season with salt and pepper and simmer the soup for 30 minutes or until the carrots are very tender.

3. Cool the soup and transfer to a food processor or blender and process until smooth.

4. Return the soup to the casserole. Add the cream and simmer for another 20 minutes. Correct the seasoning.

5. Serve the soup hot or at room temperature garnished with tiny fresh coriander (cilantro) leaves or a combination of fresh coriander and mint leaves.

R·E·M·A·R·K·S

If you wish the soup to have more texture, finely dice and steam an additional large carrot and add it to the soup before serving. For a slightly different texture, add the heart of a Boston lettuce, separated into leaves, to the finished soup and simmer just until wilted.

4 tablespoons unsalted butter

1 large onion peeled and finely minced

1 tablespoon dark brown sugar

½ teaspoon ground coriander

1 tablespoon imported curry powder, preferably Madras

¼ teaspoon ground cardamom

Large pinch of freshly grated nutmeg

1 pound carrots, trimmed, peeled, and cubed

2 medium all-purpose potatoes, peeled and cubed

6 cups Chicken Stock (page 37) or bouillon

Salt and freshly ground black pepper

½–¾ cup heavy cream

GARNISH

Tiny fresh coriander (cilantro) leaves

Tiny mint leaves

SERVES 6

Carrot Clafoutis

4 medium carrots, trimmed and
   peeled
3 tablespoons unsalted butter
3 tablespoons dark brown sugar
Salt and freshly ground white
   pepper
3 tablespoons water
4 large eggs
¼ cup all-purpose flour
1 cup milk
3 tablespoons unsalted butter,
   melted
Large grinding of nutmeg
1–2 teaspoons grated orange rind

SERVES 6

Clafoutis is a country pudding that has the texture of a custardy tart but has no crust. It is usually combined with seasonal fruit, such as cherries or plums, but is equally delicious made with carrots and is a great accompaniment to roast turkey or duck.

P·R·E·P·A·R·A·T·I·O·N

1. Preheat oven to 350°F.

2. Cut the carrots in half lengthwise and then cut crosswise into ¼-inch slices (half-moons).

3. In a heavy 10-inch skillet, melt 3 tablespoons butter over medium heat. Add the carrots and sprinkle with 1 tablespoon brown sugar. Cook for 3–5 minutes until lightly browned. Season with salt and pepper. Reduce heat, add the water, cover, and cook 6–8 minutes longer or until tender. If all the liquid has not evaporated, remove the cover, raise the heat, and cook until the liquid has evaporated and the carrots are glazed. Set aside.

4. In a food processor or blender combine the eggs, flour, milk, and melted butter. Process until smooth. Season with salt, pepper, nutmeg, and orange rind.

5. Place the carrots in a buttered 9-inch porcelain quiche pan. Top with the egg/milk mixture, making sure that the carrots are evenly dispersed.

6. Set the quiche pan in a shallow baking dish. Fill the baking dish with boiling water to come halfway up the sides of the quiche pan. Set in the center of the preheated oven and bake for 25–30 minutes or until the custard is set and a toothpick when inserted comes out clean.

7. When the clafoutis is done, remove from the oven and preheat broiler. Sprinkle the remaining brown sugar over the top. Place under broiler 6 inches from the source of heat until the brown sugar becomes crisp (the sugar does not really melt). Be careful not to burn the custard.

8. Serve hot as a first course cut into wedges, like a pie.

Puree of Carrots with Crème Fraîche & Honey

P·R·E·P·A·R·A·T·I·O·N

1. Bring lightly salted water to a boil in a vegetable steamer. Add the carrots, cover, and steam for 15 minutes or until very tender.

2. Transfer the carrots to a food processor or blender and puree until smooth.

3. Place the carrot puree in a 2-quart saucepan over medium heat and stir constantly for 2 minutes to remove excess water from the puree. Add the honey and granulated sugar and stir until honey and sugar are dissolved.

4. Add the crème fraîche and butter and stir until smooth. Season with salt, a large grinding of white pepper, and a pinch of nutmeg. Serve hot.

R·E·M·A·R·K·S

The carrot puree can be made ahead of time and kept warm in a double boiler.

V·A·R·I·A·T·I·O·N

The puree is equally delicious with 2 tablespoons dark brown sugar substituted for the honey.

2 pounds medium carrots (about 12–14), peeled, trimmed, and cut into ½-inch pieces

Salt

2 tablespoons honey

1 teaspoon granulated sugar

¼ cup Crème Fraîche (page 57)

3–4 tablespoons unsalted butter, softened

Freshly ground white pepper

Pinch of freshly grated nutmeg

SERVES 5–6

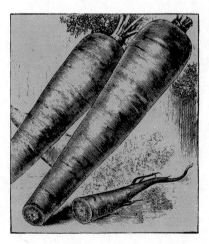

Roast Pork with Carrots & Prunes in Sweet Port Wine Sauce

THE PORK

A 2½-pound pork butt, boned, rolled, and tied

Coarse salt

Freshly ground black pepper

1 tablespoon fresh thyme

1 large clove garlic, peeled and mashed to a paste

2 tablespoons unsalted butter

1 tablespoon corn oil

2 small onions, peeled and cut in half

2 cups hot beef bouillon

THE CARROTS AND PRUNES

16–20 prunes

¼ cup port wine

2 tablespoons unsalted butter

6–7 medium carrots (about 1 pound), trimmed, peeled, and cut into pieces ½ by ½ by 1 inch

Salt and freshly ground black pepper

1 teaspoon granulated sugar

2 tablespoons dark brown sugar

1 teaspoon arrowroot mixed with a little cold bouillon

GARNISH

Sprigs of fresh curly parsley

SERVES 4–5

P·R·E·P·A·R·A·T·I·O·N

1. Preheat oven to 375°F.

2. Soak the prunes for *the sauce*: bring water to a boil in a small saucepan. Add the prunes, cook for 5 minutes, and drain. Combine with port wine in a small bowl. Set aside.

3. Dry the pork butt thoroughly on paper towels. Season with coarse salt, pepper, and thyme. Make tiny slits along the bottom of the roast and insert bits of the garlic paste.

4. Heat the butter and oil over medium heat in a large heavy skillet, preferably cast iron or a flameproof baking dish. Add the pork roast and brown nicely on all sides; regulate the heat so as not to burn the fat. When the pork is browned on all sides, add the onions, cut side down, to the skillet together with ¼ cup bouillon. Place in center of the preheated oven and roast 1½ hours or until it reaches an internal temperature of 160°F, adding 2–3 tablespoons stock every 15 minutes and basting the roast with pan juices.

5. While the pork is roasting, *prepare the carrots*: in a medium skillet melt 2 tablespoons butter over medium heat. Add the carrots, season with salt, pepper, and the granulated sugar. Cook for 3–4 minutes. Add ¼ cup of the bouillon to the skillet, cover, and simmer until tender (about 10–12 minutes).

6. Add the brown sugar to the skillet and cook until the sugar has melted and carrots are nicely glazed. Reserve.

7. Drain the prunes, reserving the port.

8. When the roast is done, transfer it to a cutting board.

9. Carefully degrease and remove the pan juices. Place the skillet or baking dish over high heat, add the reserved port, bring to a boil, and reduce to a glaze. Return the pan juices along with the remaining bouillon, bring to a boil, and whisk in enough of the arrowroot mixture so that the sauce coats a spoon. Add the carrot mixture and prunes and just heat through. Taste and correct the seasoning, adding a large grinding of black pepper.

10. Slice the roast thinly and place on a serving platter in a slightly overlapping pattern. Spoon the sauce over the meat and garnish with sprigs of fresh parsley and serve at once.

Creamy Carrot & Cabbage Slaw

P·R·E·P·A·R·A·T·I·O·N

1. Place each of the cabbages in a separate colander or strainer. Sprinkle each with 1 teaspoon salt and let drain for 1 hour.

2. With your hands squeeze out as much moisture as you can from the cabbages. Set aside.

3. In a large bowl combine the mayonnaise, sour cream, cider vinegar, sugar, and dill. Season with salt and pepper and whisk until smooth. Add the red and green cabbages, carrots, red onion, green pepper, and diced apple. Toss to coat well with the dressing, cover, and refrigerate overnight.

4. The next day, bring the slaw back to room temperature. Taste and correct the seasoning, adding more vinegar if necessary, and serve.

¾ pound red cabbage, cored and very thinly sliced

¾ pound green cabbage, cored and very thinly sliced

Salt

¾ cup Homemade Mayonnaise (page 13)

⅓ cup sour cream

2 tablespoons cider vinegar

2 tablespoons granulated sugar

2 tablespoons finely minced fresh dill

Freshly ground black pepper

3 medium carrots, peeled and finely shredded

1 small red onion, peeled and finely diced

1 medium green bell pepper, cored, seeded, and finely diced

1 large Golden Delicious apple, peeled, cored, and finely diced

SERVES 6–8

Rice Pilaf of Carrots
& Golden Raisins

1/3 cup granulated sugar

2 tablespoons water

3½ cups hot Chicken Stock
(page 37) or bouillon

5 tablespoons unsalted butter

1 medium onion, peeled and finely
minced

1½ cups long-grain rice

Salt and freshly ground white
pepper

2 medium carrots, trimmed, peeled,
and cut into ½-inch cubes

2 tablespoons golden raisins

SERVES 6

P·R·E·P·A·R·A·T·I·O·N

1. In a 2-quart saucepan combine the sugar and water. Place over high heat, bring to a boil, stir once to dissolve sugar, and continue to boil without stirring until the mixture turns a hazelnut brown. Immediately add 3 cups hot chicken broth all at once, averting your face; bring to a boil and remove from the heat. Set aside.

2. Melt 3 tablespoons butter in a 3½-quart saucepan over medium heat. Add the onion and cook until soft but not browned. Add the rice and stir until thoroughly coated with the butter. Season with salt and pepper.

3. Add the caramelized stock and bring to a boil. Reduce the heat and simmer the rice, covered, for 25–30 minutes or until tender.

4. While the rice is cooking, prepare the carrots. Melt the remaining butter in a 10-inch skillet. Add the carrots and raisins and cook for 1 minute. Add the remaining chicken broth, reduce heat, cover, and cook for 10–12 minutes or until tender. Remove the cover, raise the heat, and cook until the juices have evaporated.

5. When the rice is done, add the carrot/raisin mixture and fold gently. Taste and correct the seasoning and serve hot.

Grated Carrot & Pineapple Muffins

1. Preheat oven to 400°F. Lightly oil 3 standard-size muffin pans. Set aside.

2. In a large mixing bowl, sift together the flour, baking powder, baking soda, salt, cinnamon, and spices and reserve.

3. Combine the sugar, oil, sour cream, and eggs in a food processor and process until smooth. Add the grated carrots and pineapple and pulse two times.

4. Add the carrot/pineapple mixture to the mixing bowl containing the dry ingredients. Fold together with a large spatula until the flour just disappears. Do not overmix.

5. Spoon the batter into the prepared pans, filling each muffin tin about ¾ full. Place in the center of the preheated oven and bake for 20 minutes or until a toothpick when inserted comes out clean.

6. Remove from the oven and cool in the pans for 10 minutes. Unmold onto wire cake racks and cool completely.

2 cups all-purpose flour
2 teaspoons baking powder
1½ teaspoons baking soda
1 teaspoon salt
2 teaspoons ground cinnamon
Pinch of ground nutmeg, cloves, and allspice
2 cups granulated sugar
½ cup vegetable oil, preferably corn
½ cup sour cream
4 large eggs
2 cups grated carrots
1 can (8½ ounces) crushed pineapple, drained

MAKES 1½ DOZEN

R·E·M·A·R·K·S

If you do not have a food processor, you may add the sugar, oil, sour cream, and eggs to the dry ingredients and mix with a wooden spoon until combined. Be careful not to overmix or the muffins will be dry. The muffins are better when served the next day.

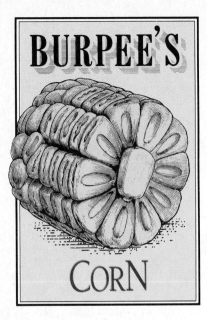

BURPEE'S

CORN

I tasted corn for the first time in the Middle East, where street vendors sell cobs straight from boiling vats as a kind of local fast food. Although the experience was interesting, I never quite understood what made corn so special until I moved to the United States. My first summer, I was introduced to the delicious "eight-row" corn grown in Pennsylvania. I was an instant convert and fresh corn has been a summer staple in my kitchen ever since.

Initially I bought corn in peak season at the supermarket. But I soon learned that corn, more than any other vegetable, ships poorly and is much better when purchased from roadside farm stands; summer after summer I searched country roads in pursuit of the freshest and juiciest cobs. My quest ended when I began growing corn in my own garden. There simply is no equal to homegrown corn picked just before dinner, boiled briefly, and then served on the cob with no more enhancement than a tab of butter and a sprinkling of salt. Corn "off the cob" is nearly as delightful. Removing the kernels is easily done with a corn cutter and creamer. The versatility of corn is far from exhausted by the recipes that follow, and leftovers can be used to add a dash of color and texture to various soups or salads.

With the new American cuisine now coming into its own, corn, the all-American staple, is used more creatively than ever in new and spectacular dishes. Aside from such tempting all-American classics as corn spoon bread, corn pudding, and corn fritters, I think you will enjoy experimenting with corn in a sauté of shrimp or in a contemporary roasted pepper and corn dressing.

S·T·O·R·A·G·E

Ears picked early in the day or bought at a farm stand should be refrigerated immediately, preferably in plastic bags, without removing the husks. Corn that can't be cooked the same day should be saved for soups and chowders. I always try to cook corn the day I get it even if I don't intend to use it right away. I find it best to remove the corn from its cooking water and store it in the

refrigerator. The kernels may become a bit soggy, but they still taste wonderful in a mixed pasta salad or as an addition to a flavorful minestrone or other summer soup. To freeze any garden surplus, it is best to blanch the corn, on the cob, for about two minutes. When completely cool, pack in small freezer bags.

G·A·R·D·E·N·I·N·G

Freshly picked corn is such a joy that even in a relatively small garden, it's worth finding some space for it. Plants must get full sun all day and should be planted along the garden's northern edge so they won't shade shorter crops. Since corn depends on wind for pollination, it's better to plant at least four short rows side by side than to plant one long row. This way, ears are more likely to produce full sets of kernels.

Corn seeds germinate best when soil becomes warm (65°F) in mid to late spring. Sometimes I just can't wait to set the seed into the ground, but if it's a little earlier or cooler than usual, I coat the seeds with a fungicide such as Captan. I follow my initial sowing of early, mid, and late season varieties with another sowing of a late variety in about three weeks. By midsummer the first ears are ready for picking. Harvests continue into September, when cool nights seem to make maturing sweet corn even sweeter.

Extra-Sweet, Sugar Extender, Everlasting Heritage (or E.H.), and Illini are designations for many modern corn varieties, all considerably higher in sugar content than the more typical hybrid corn—up to three times as sweet when picked. Moreover, they hold their sweetness for much longer periods than typical hybrids. Whereas the typical corn turns its sugar to starch within a few days in storage, new varieties such as "How Sweet It Is" stay sweet and tender in the refrigerator, but not on the stalk, for up to two weeks. Everlasting Heritage types are the ones that keep very well on the stalk for an extended harvest. Extra-Sweet and Illini types need to be isolated from other varieties so the pollen doesn't cross, but E.H. and Sugar Extender types can be planted without regard to what's in your neighbor's yard—a big advantage for home gardeners.

It seems to me, though, that these new kinds offer more to the farmer who ships corn to market than to the home gardener, who can usually eat what he or she picks within a day or two of harvesting. So I recommend that you do as I do: Grow the varieties that taste best to *you*. Not everyone likes the candy sweetness of some of the new varieties or the crunchy texture that has replaced the creaminess of the older kinds.

So many new varieties are introduced each year that few of us have a chance to decide on a favorite before another comes along. In my region, and through much of the East, Silver Queen, a white corn introduced in the early '60s, is considered the paragon of corn, so popular that roadside stands and produce markets call all their white corn Silver Queen, although it may in fact be something else.

H·A·R·V·E·S·T·I·N·G

Probably the trickiest thing about growing corn is knowing when to pick it. Some people judge corn ripe when the tassels turn brown. I find the hand more reliable than the eye. If the tip end inside the husk is more or less rounded, the ear is ready. A pointed tip means the end kernels haven't matured yet. To pick, simply pull down the ear and twist.

CHICKEN STOCK

In large casserole, combine two 3-pound chickens cut in eight pieces, 2 scraped carrots, 2 stalks celery, 2 leeks, and 3 to 4 sprigs Italian parsley. Add 12 cups cold water. Season with a teaspoon salt. Bring to a boil, reduce heat, and simmer for 1 hour and 30 minutes. Strain stock. Chill overnight. The next day, skim all fat. Bring back to a boil. Cool and refrigerate or freeze in covered jars. Makes 3 quarts.

Variations: For beef or veal stock, substitute 4 to 5 pounds of meaty beef bones for chicken. You may also use a combination of veal and beef or veal and chicken, which will give the stock a more gelatinous consistency.

R·E·C·I·P·E·S

Egg "Flower" & Corn Soup 38

Summer's Best Corn Chowder 39

Corn & Zucchini Fritters 40

Sour Cream Corn Bread 41

Corn & Cheddar Cheese Omelettes 42

Corn-Studded Polenta 43

Corn Salad Mexicane 44

Roasted Pepper & Corn Dressing 45

Sauté of Shrimp & Corn Indienne 46

Southern Fried Chicken Wings with Spicy Corn Relish 47

Egg "Flower" & Corn Soup

6 cups Chicken Stock (page 37) or
    bouillon

1 teaspoon granulated sugar

1½ cups fresh corn kernels (about
    2–3 ears)

1 tablespoon cornstarch mixed with
    a little cold stock

3 ounces snow peas, strings removed
    and cut into a fine julienne

2 large eggs, lightly beaten

4 medium scallions, trimmed and
    thinly sliced

1 teaspoon sesame oil

Salt and freshly ground black
    pepper

SERVES 4

P·R·E·P·A·R·A·T·I·O·N

1. In a 4-quart saucepan combine the stock and sugar. Bring to a boil, add the corn, reduce heat, and simmer, partially covered, for 4–6 minutes or until corn is tender.

2. Bring soup back to a boil, add the cornstarch mixture, and whisk until the soup clears.

3. Add the snow peas and cook for 1 minute. Slowly pour in the beaten eggs in a circular motion. Do not stir. Turn off the heat. Add the scallions and sesame oil and stir gently, being careful not to break the egg "flower." Taste and correct the seasoning and serve at once.

Summer's Best Corn Chowder

P·R·E·P·A·R·A·T·I·O·N

1. Scrape corn off the cobs with scraper or sharp knife and reserve. (You should have about 2 cups.)

2. Bring lightly salted water to a boil in a medium saucepan. Add the sugar. Add the corn and cook for 5–7 minutes or until just tender. Drain and set aside.

3 In a 4-quart casserole heat the butter. Add the bacon and sauté until lightly browned. Remove with a slotted spoon and set aside.

4. Discard all but 3 tablespoons of fat from the casserole. Add the onion and peppers and simmer the mixture for 3–4 minutes or until soft. Add the tomatoes and simmer for another 3–4 minutes.

5. Add the flour and blend thoroughly. Add the stock and cream. Bring to a boil, reduce heat, and season with salt and pepper.

6. Return the corn and bacon to the soup. Add the zucchini and simmer for 25 minutes. Taste and correct the seasoning and keep warm.

7. Just before serving, add the parsley or garden cress leaves and let the leaves wilt in the soup. Serve hot accompanied by crusty French bread.

2 large ears of fresh corn

Salt

1 teaspoon granulated sugar

1 tablespoon unsalted butter

4 ounces lean bacon, diced

1 large onion, peeled and finely minced

1 small green bell pepper and 1 small red bell pepper, cored, seeded, and finely diced

3 large ripe tomatoes, peeled, seeded, and finely chopped

2 tablespoons all-purpose flour

2 cups Chicken Stock (page 37) or bouillon

2½ cups light cream

1 small zucchini, trimmed and diced

Freshly ground black pepper

GARNISH

½ cup tiny parsley leaves or garden cress

SERVES 6

Corn & Zucchini Fritters

1 cup cooked corn kernels, lightly
  minced

5 tablespoons all-purpose flour

4 large eggs

½ cup heavy cream

2 teaspoons grated raw onion

Salt and freshly ground white
  pepper to taste

3 tablespoons finely grated zucchini
  skin

Corn oil for sautéeing

MAKES ABOUT 25 CREPES

P·R·E·P·A·R·A·T·I·O·N

1. Thoroughly combine all ingredients except oil in a medium bowl and blend well. Let the batter rest for 30 minutes.

2. In a 10-inch nonstick skillet heat 3 tablespoons oil over medium heat. When hot, drop the batter by tablespoonfuls into the hot oil, without crowding the pan, and fry until nicely browned, about 1 minute per side. Cook in batches of 4–5, adjusting the heat so the crepes do not brown too quickly and adding more corn oil to the skillet if necessary.

3. Remove with a slotted spoon to a double layer of paper towels to drain. Serve hot as a vegetable with roast or grilled meats.

R·E·M·A·R·K·S

Since these are not crisp fritters, they can be kept warm, covered with foil, in a 200°F oven.

Sour Cream Corn Bread

1. Sift together the cornmeal, flour, sugar, baking powder, and salt into a large mixing bowl and set aside.

2. In another large mixing bowl combine the eggs, sour cream, and milk. Whisk until well blended. Reserve.

3. Generously butter a heavy 9-inch-square cake pan. Place in the center of the oven and preheat to 400°F.

4. While oven is heating, melt the butter in a small heavy saucepan. Add the corn kernels and cook over medium-low heat until tender, about 5–7 minutes.

5. Whisk the corn and butter into the egg/milk mixture. Add the sifted dry ingredients. Stir with a wooden spoon until just incorporated. Do not overmix or corn bread will be dry.

6. Remove the cake pan from the oven. Pour the batter into the hot pan and return to the center of the preheated oven. Bake for 20–25 minutes or until golden. A cake tester when inserted should come out clean.

7. Remove from the oven and let cool slightly. Cut into squares and serve warm.

1¼ cups coarse yellow cornmeal
¾ cup all-purpose flour
3 tablespoons granulated sugar
2½ teaspoons baking powder
1 teaspoon salt
3 large eggs
½ cup sour cream
¾ cup whole milk
6 tablespoons unsalted butter
1 cup fresh corn kernels, lightly
  minced

SERVES 8–10

Corn & Cheddar Cheese Omelettes

It is best to make omelettes individually, that is, one per person, each made with 2 or 3 eggs. The following recipe is for 2 individual omelettes.

4 tablespoons unsalted butter

¾ cup fresh corn kernels (about 1 ear)

2 tablespoons water

Salt

Pinch of granulated sugar

2 tablespoons finely minced scallions

5–6 large eggs, lightly beaten

Freshly ground black pepper

Dash of Tabasco sauce

⅔ cup finely shredded sharp white cheddar cheese, preferably Vermont

2 teaspoons finely diced, roasted, and peeled jalapeño pepper (page 65)

GARNISH

Bowl of sour cream

Bowl of Grilled Tomato Salsa (page 103)

SERVES 2

P·R·E·P·A·R·A·T·I·O·N

1. In a small heavy skillet melt 2 tablespoons butter over medium heat. Add the corn, water, pinch of salt, and pinch of sugar. Cover and braise the corn for 5–7 minutes until just tender. Remove the cover, raise heat, and cook until juices have evaporated. Remove the pan from the heat, stir in the scallions, and set aside.

2. In a large bowl combine the eggs and corn mixture. Mix until well blended. Season with salt, pepper, and Tabasco sauce.

3. In a heavy 8-inch omelette pan, preferably nonstick, heat 1 tablespoon butter over medium-high heat. When the butter is very hot and the foam begins to subside, add half the egg mixture. Cook the eggs for 1–2 minutes to let settle, then stir with the back of a fork until the eggs start to form a thick mass. Sprinkle with half the cheese and diced jalapeño. Tilt the pan away from you and with the aid of a spatula fold ⅓ of the omelette farthest from you onto itself and toward the center of the pan. Prod the part closest to you, pushing the omelette toward the far end of the skillet. Jerk the pan roughly so that the omelette completely rolls onto itself.

4. Turn the omelette onto a plate and keep warm. Butter the skillet again and make the second omelette in the same manner.

5. Serve at once with a dollop of sour cream and Grilled Tomato Salsa.

Corn-Studded Polenta

1. Start by preparing *the corn.* In a medium skillet, melt the butter over medium heat. Add the corn and toss with the butter. Add the water, salt, and sugar. Cover and braise 5–7 minutes or until tender. Remove the cover, raise heat, and cook until all the juices have evaporated. Set aside.

2. *The Polenta:* In a 4-quart saucepan bring the water and 1 tablespoon salt to a boil. Reduce the heat and sprinkle the cornmeal a little at a time into the water, whisking constantly to avoid lumping. It will take about 20 minutes until all the cornmeal has been added to the water. Stir in the milk and reserved corn, cover, and cook over low heat for another 10–15 minutes until cornmeal is tender.

3. Remove the polenta from the heat and stir in the butter and Parmesan. Taste and correct the seasoning. Serve in deep individual bowls, topped with Spicy Sauté of Peppers and Sausages (page 76) and sprinkled with Parmesan or simply sprinkled with Parmesan as a first course or accompaniment to roast lamb or pork.

THE CORN

2 tablespoons unsalted butter

2 cups fresh corn kernels (about 2–3 ears)

2 tablespoons water

Pinch salt

Pinch granulated sugar

THE POLENTA

6½ cups water

1 tablespoon salt

2 cups coarse yellow cornmeal

2–3 tablespoons whole milk

6 tablespoons unsalted butter

½ cup freshly grated Parmesan cheese

Salt and freshly ground black pepper

SERVES 6

When the polenta is done stir in 3 ounces mild goat cheese, crumbled, and 2 tablespoons fresh thyme and/or marjoram leaves together with the butter. Eliminate the Parmesan cheese.

Corn Salad Mexicane

½ pound medium shrimp

Salt

5 tablespoons olive oil

2 tablespoons red wine vinegar

2 large cloves garlic, peeled and mashed

Freshly ground black pepper

4 cups fresh corn kernels (about 4–5 ears)

Juice of 1 lime

1 small red onion, peeled and finely minced

2 fresh jalapeño peppers, roasted, peeled (page 65), and diced

1 medium red bell pepper, cored, seeded, and finely diced

2 tablespoons finely minced fresh coriander (cilantro)

Pinch of cayenne pepper

GARNISH

Sprigs of fresh coriander (cilantro)

Halved cherry tomatoes

SERVES 6

P·R·E·P·A·R·A·T·I·O·N

1. In a small saucepan, bring salted water to a boil. Add the shrimp and cook until just pink and opaque (2–3 minutes). Run the shrimp under cold water to stop further cooking. Peel and cut into ½-inch pieces. Set aside.

2. Combine 2 tablespoons olive oil, vinegar, and crushed garlic clove in a medium mixing bowl. Add the diced shrimp, season with salt and pepper, toss, and marinate for 1 hour at room temperature. Drain, discard garlic, and reserve shrimp.

3. Bring water to a boil in a medium saucepan. Add the corn and cook for 5–7 minutes or until tender. Drain and set aside.

4. In a large mixing bowl combine the remaining olive oil and vinegar, lime juice, mashed clove of garlic, and minced red onion. Whisk until well blended. Add the drained shrimp, cooked corn, cayenne pepper, red bell pepper, and coriander. Toss well with the vinaigrette and season with salt, pepper, and a pinch of cayenne. Chill for 2 hours.

5. At serving time, bring salad back to room temperature. Taste and correct the seasoning, adding more oil and vinegar if necessary. Garnish with sprigs of coriander and halved cherry tomatoes.

V·A·R·I·A·T·I·O·N

As part of a light luncheon you may spoon the salad into hollowed-out tomatoes. Cut a ¼-inch slice off each tomato bottom (the end opposite the stem end) and reserve. Carefully scoop out the pulp and seeds, leaving a good ⅓ inch of shell. (Discard the seeds and reserve the pulp for soups, stocks, and sauces.) Sprinkle the shells with coarse salt and place upside down on a double layer of paper towels to drain for 30 minutes to 1 hour. Fill the tomatoes with corn salad. Top each with the reserved tomato cap and a sprig of coriander. Line a serving platter with lettuce leaves, place the tomatoes on top, and serve at room temperature with a loaf of crusty French bread.

Roasted Pepper & Corn Dressing

This is more a sauce than a dressing. It makes a lovely topping for a ripe avocado or steamed asparagus, or as a sauce with grilled shrimp. It keeps well for up to 10 days if stored in a covered jar in the refrigerator, but be sure not to add the garlic to the sauce until an hour or so before serving.

P·R·E·P·A·R·A·T·I·O·N

1. Place the red pepper, vinegar, and oil in a food processor or blender and process until smooth.

2. Transfer the puree to a bowl, add the crème fraîche or sour cream. Season with salt, pepper, mashed garlic, and a pinch of cayenne and whisk until well blended.

3. Add the corn kernels, basil, and optional coriander; blend well. Taste and correct the seasoning. Refrigerate the dressing for 1 hour before serving; bring it back to room temperature before serving.

1 large red bell pepper, roasted, peeled (page 65), and diced

2 tablespoons red wine vinegar

6 tablespoons olive oil

½ cup Crème Fraîche (page 57) or sour cream

Salt and freshly ground black pepper

1 medium clove garlic, peeled and mashed

Pinch of cayenne pepper

¾ cup cooked corn kernels (about 1–2 ears)

2 tablespoons finely julienned fresh basil leaves

Optional: 2 tablespoons finely minced fresh coriander (cilantro)

MAKES ABOUT 2 CUPS

Sauté of Shrimp & Corn Indienne

5 cloves garlic, peeled and finely
  minced

1-inch piece gingerroot, peeled and
  finely minced

3 tablespoons tomato paste

1 tablespoon water

¼ teaspoon turmeric

Salt and freshly ground black
  pepper

1 pound small fresh shrimp, peeled

3–4 tablespoons olive oil,
  preferably extra-virgin

2 small fresh or dry cayenne
  peppers, broken

Coarse salt

1 small green bell pepper, cored,
  seeded, and diced (about ½ cup)

1 cup fresh corn kernels

1 small zucchini, trimmed and cut
  into julienne strips ¼ by ¼ by 2
  inches

1 tablespoon lemon juice

¼ cup finely minced fresh
  coriander (cilantro)

SERVES 4–6

P·R·E·P·A·R·A·T·I·O·N

1. In a food processor or blender, combine the garlic, ginger, tomato paste, water, and turmeric. Puree until smooth. Season with salt and pepper and set aside.

2. Dry the shrimp thoroughly on paper towels.

3. In a large skillet, heat the oil over high heat. Add the cayenne peppers and cook until dark; discard. Sprinkle the shrimp with coarse salt and add to the skillet. Cook for 2 minutes, shaking the pan back and forth, until the shrimp turn bright pink and are lightly browned; do not overcook. Remove the shrimp with a slotted spoon to a side dish. Reserve.

4. Reduce the heat, add the green pepper, corn, and zucchini, and cook for 1 minute. Add the tomato paste mixture, lemon juice, and coriander and cook for 2–3 minutes, stirring constantly. The vegetables should still be crisp.

5. Return the shrimp to the skillet and toss to coat with the vegetable mixture and just heat through. Taste and correct the seasoning. Serve at once directly from the skillet accompanied by a Pilaf of Zucchini with Tomato Fondue (page 113).

Southern Fried Chicken Wings with Spicy Corn Relish

P·R·E·P·A·R·A·T·I·O·N

1. Bring plenty of water to a boil in a large pot. Add the ears of corn and cook for 10 minutes. Drain. Remove the kernels from the cob with a sharp knife; you should have about 3 cups. Reserve.

2. In a 10-inch skillet heat the olive oil over medium heat. Add the ginger slices and cook until browned. Remove and discard. Add the jalapeño pepper and red and green peppers. Cook for 30 seconds. Add the corn and rice wine or vinegar/sugar combination and cook until the wine is reduced to a glaze. Season with salt and pepper and set aside.

3. Season the wing pieces with salt and pepper. Dredge lightly in flour, shaking off the excess.

4. In a large heavy skillet or chicken fryer heat oil to a depth of ½ inch over medium-high heat. When hot add the chicken wings and cook, turning the pieces for 10–12 mintues until crisp and nicely browned on all sides. Regulate the heat so as not to burn the wings.

5. Remove the wings from the skillet with kitchen tongs and place on paper towels to drain. Serve hot with corn relish.

THE CORN RELISH

4 ears of fresh corn, husks removed

½ cup olive oil

3 slices fresh ginger, each about the size of a quarter

1 teaspoon or more to taste finely diced jalapeño pepper

1 medium red bell pepper and 1 medium green bell pepper, cored, seeded, and finely diced

1 cup syrupy rice wine, preferably Mirin, or 3 tablespoons cider vinegar plus 1 tablespoon granulated sugar

Salt and freshly ground black pepper

THE CHICKEN WINGS

12–16 chicken wings, each cut at joint into 2 pieces (discard tips or reserve for stocks)

Salt and freshly ground black pepper

Flour for dredging

Corn oil for frying

SERVES 4–6

BURPEE'S
CUCUMBERS

Nothing is quite as satisfying and refreshing on a hot summer day as the taste of the cucumber. Easy to grow, wonderful to have on hand throughout summer and early fall, cucumbers lend their crisp juicy flavor to many soups and salads.

I often marvel at the tremendous appeal the cucumber has throughout the world. The Scandinavian smorgasbord would not be complete without cucumber salads, nor would the artfully decorated Danish open sandwich. The Viennese serve a sweet cucumber salad much as we do coleslaw—it is considered a "national" salad. The Greeks use cucumbers in combination with yogurt, feta cheese and mint, while the Indian "Raita" cucumber salad acts as a cooling counterpoint to fiery curries and spices.

Several years ago, while on a trip in Russia, I found myself on a bus in Moscow on a hot July day. I was amazed to see several people, including children, snack on small, unpeeled cucumbers. They reminded me of Americans with Granola bars. What a great idea! Later on that same trip I found that while restaurant menus listed a variety of vegetables, only one was ever available: cucumbers. It was on that Russian journey that I was introduced to the wonderful soup in which diced cucumber is combined with sour cream, buttermilk, lots of minced dill and diced shrimp. It has since become one of my favorite summer appetizers.

With the recent rise in popularity of burpless (or "gourmet") varieties, the cucumber now is being used quite creatively in many warm preparations as well. Some of the finest restaurants in France cut the long and slender flesh, skin intact, into olive-like shapes, which are then braised in a little water, butter and a pinch of sugar. Sweet yet mellow, the results are a perfect accompaniment to fish—salmon, snapper and scallops in particular. And more and more cooks are discovering that hot cucumbers combine amazingly well with almost any herb, allowing the cook to experiment with various flavors in the summer kitchen.

Most cucumbers found in American supermarkets throughout the year lack crispness, are extremely seedy and, because they

are usually waxed, have skin that is inedible. When you grow your own cucumbers, peeling and seeding are not required but are merely a matter of personal taste. If garden cukes are picked regularly on the young side, they will have small edible seeds and crunchy, flavorful skins. I peel most homegrown cucumbers but seed only the larger ones and those to be combined with leafy greens in salads or in hot preparations.

In most cases, raw cucumbers release a tremendous amount of liquid and, when added to tossed salads, will water down the dressing. So, it is best to first salt sliced cucumbers, and then drain them for an hour in a colander.

Since cucumber vines tend to produce more fruit than you might care to pick, I find the average kitchen garden needs only a few plants of regular or burpless slicing varieties, a few plants of a pickling variety, plus one of the small gherkins. I especially like West India Gherkin pickled either in a sweet brine or in a sharp vinegar brine much like French cornichons, which are delicious with boiled meats, baked ham or country pâté. In France, cornichons are served as commonly as our dills; you can make them out of tiny fruits of any pickling variety.

I have been making more and more use of the pickling varieties—they are firmer and drier than salad-type cucumbers when eaten fresh, though somewhat more bitter—but I prefer the burpless cucumber. Here is a perfect vegetable. It is excellent for sautéeing and braising; finely sliced, it makes a wonderful garnish; and it adds delicious taste and crisp texture to salads without watering down a dressing. And of course, burpless varieties are easier to digest than conventional ones.

S · T · O · R · A · G · E

Because of their moisture content, cucumbers must be refrigerated and kept from drying out. It is best to place the fruit in perforated plastic bags in the vegetable bin, or in brown paper bags near the bottom of the refrigerator. This way, cucumbers will keep for four to six days and often longer.

Cucumber vines are extremely sensitive to the cold, so spring planting should be delayed until the soil warms up to about 60 to 70°F. You will still reap a good harvest of fruit because cucumbers take as little as fifty-five days to mature. Since my growing season is short, I get an early start by germinating seeds indoors in peat pots about a month before planting time. I plant three seeds per pot and later snip away the two weakest seedlings. Peat pots are ideal for cucumbers because the seedlings can be transplanted to the garden—pot and all—without disturbing their particularly sensitive roots.

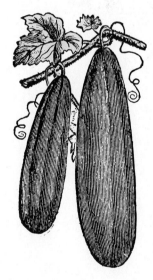

Untended, the vines will eventually sprawl six feet or more along the ground. In a small garden a practical approach is to train the plants on fences, trellises or garden netting. The upright plants not only will save space but will produce fruits that are straighter and more attractive than those from trailing plants. Another good idea is to grow some "bush" cucumbers, relatively new varieties whose short, compact vines require about one-third the space of conventional cucumbers.

The traditional way to plant cucumbers is in two-foot-wide mounds, called "hills," which are built to about a foot high with the addition of well-rotted manure or compost. I find, however, that trellised vines and bush varieties do quite well in ordinary rows. Rich, well-drained soil is essential for good productivity, so add compost liberally and apply Burpee fertilizer at planting time. Before planting, I roll plastic mulch over the rows where vines will be allowed to sprawl. The plastic sheeting traps warmth in the soil, conserves moisture, smothers weeds and protects fruit from soil-borne diseases and insects. You might want to shield seeds and young plants against chilly spring nights with translucent Hotkaps; so protected, seeds germinate and grow quite quickly.

There is no cause for alarm if, at first, flowers appear but do not set fruit. Most cucumber varieties have both male and female flowers on the same vine. Frequently, the first blossoms to unfurl are males. Before long the vines will start producing females, and fruit will be seen soon thereafter. Some of the newer and highest yielding varieties are "gynoecious"—that is, they have female flowers only. Male flowers are needed to pollinate the females, so seed packets always include a few seeds of a conventional variety. Gynoecious varieties yield amazingly large crops, and many are also early-bearing and disease-resistant. Among the best and most popular is Burpee Hybrid II, a new gynoecious version of America's first hybrid cucumber, introduced in 1945.

Since cucumbers are pollinated by bees, any necessary pesticides should be used late in the day after the bees have returned to the safety of their hives.

H · A · R · V · E · S · T · I · N · G

Cucumbers, like beans, should be picked young and often. If fruits are left on the vine to mature, the plants' productivity will quickly taper off and cease. Most slicing cucumbers can be picked as small as six inches, and must be picked before the skin starts to yellow and the seeds to harden. Pickling types can be picked at any stage, depending on whether you want sweet midget pickles or large dills. Use a sharp knife or pruning shears to harvest cucumbers.

R · E · C · I · P · E · S

Overnight Crunchy Pickles 53

Ever-So-Sweet Viennese Cucumber Salad 54

Minted Middle Eastern Cucumber Salad 55

Zesty Mixed Cucumber & Sour Cream Dip 56

Braised Carrots & Cucumbers with Tarragon Cream 57

Sauté of Chicken Breasts in Lemon & Cucumber Sauce 58

Cucumber Boats with Goat Cheese & Summer Herbs 59

Fillets of Sole in Cucumber & Tomato Sauce 60

Cucumber, Shrimp & Mushroom Salad in Mustard Dill
    Mayonnaise 61

Overnight Crunchy Pickles

P · R · E · P · A · R · A · T · I · O · N

1. Cut each cucumber in half lengthwise and then cut each half into 4 lengthwise strips. Cut the onion crosswise into ⅓-inch slices and separate into rings. Alternate layers of cucumbers and onions in a large glass bowl. Set aside.

2. In a medium saucepan combine the vinegar, sugar, spices, salt, and cream of tartar. Bring to just a simmer, stirring with a wooden spoon until sugar is completely dissolved. Do not boil.

3. Pour the mixture over the cucumbers and onions and toss. Cover and refrigerate for 24 hours, tossing from time to time. Serve chilled.

6 medium cucumbers, unpeeled

1 large onion or Bermuda onion,
    peeled

1½ cups white vinegar

1½ cups granulated sugar

4 tablespoons mixed pickling spices

1 tablespoon salt

¼ teaspoon cream of tartar

MAKES 48 PICKLES

Ever-So-Sweet Viennese Cucumber Salad

2 pounds cucumbers
Coarse salt
3 tablespoons white wine vinegar
6 tablespoons peanut or corn oil
1½ tablespoons granulated sugar
3 medium scallions, trimmed and
   finely sliced
Freshly ground white pepper

SERVES 6

P·R·E·P·A·R·A·T·I·O·N

1. Peel the cucumbers and slice thinly. Place in a colander and sprinkle with coarse salt. Let the cucumbers drain for 1 hour.

2. Combine the vinegar, peanut or corn oil, sugar, and scallions in a bowl and whisk the dressing until the sugar is dissolved. Add the cucumbers, season with pepper, and toss well. Refrigerate for 2–4 hours before serving.

R·E·M·A·R·K·S

If the cucumbers are large and seedy, cut in half lengthwise and with a grapefruit spoon remove the seeds. In this case, the cucumbers do not need to be salted.

BEURRE MANIÉ

Combine 1 tablespoon soft, unsalted butter with 1 tablespoon all-purpose flour in small bowl. Work mixture with fork until smooth. Chill until ready to use. Recipe can be tripled or quadrupled (or made in large quantities).

Minted Middle Eastern Cucumber Salad

1. Place the cucumber slices in a colander. Sprinkle with 1 tablespoon vinegar and a large sprinkling of salt. Let drain for 45 minutes.

2. While the cucumbers are draining, combine the yogurt, olive oil, remaining vinegar, scallions, and mint. Add the cumin, turmeric, and garlic and season with salt and pepper. Whisk until well blended. Set aside.

3. Dry the cucumber slices thoroughly on paper towels and place in a glass bowl. Pour the dressing over them and toss gently. Chill the salad for 2 hours.

4. Just before serving garnish with sprigs of mint and serve as an accompaniment to roast or curried lamb.

4 large cucumbers, peeled, seeded, and cut crosswise into ½-inch slices

2 tablespoons white wine vinegar

Coarse salt

1 cup yogurt

2 tablespoons olive oil

3 tablespoons finely minced scallions

4 tablespoons finely minced fresh mint

½ teaspoon ground cumin

¼ teaspoon turmeric

1 large clove garlic, peeled and mashed

Freshly ground black pepper

GARNISH

Sprigs of fresh mint

SERVES 4–6

Zesty Mixed Cucumber & Sour Cream Dip

4 pickling cucumbers (4–5 inches
   long), peeled and finely diced

2 small dill pickles (gherkins),
   about 3 inches long, finely diced

¼ cup finely minced scallions

1 medium clove garlic, peeled and
   mashed

1 tablespoon red wine vinegar

½ cup sour cream

¼ cup Homemade Mayonnaise
   (page 13)

Salt and freshly ground black
   pepper

MAKES 1½ CUPS

P·R·E·P·A·R·A·T·I·O·N

1. Combine all ingredients in a small bowl and mix well. Season with salt and pepper, cover, and let stand at room temperature for 1–2 hours to develop flavor.

2. Serve with an assortment of spring vegetables as a crudité.

Braised Carrots & Cucumbers with Tarragon Cream

P·R·E·P·A·R·A·T·I·O·N

1. Place the cucumbers in a colander. Sprinkle with salt and let drain for 30 minutes. Dry thoroughly on paper towels and set aside.

2. In a medium skillet melt 2 tablespoons butter over medium heat. Add the carrots and season with a pinch of sugar and a pinch of salt. Toss in the butter and cook for 3 minutes. Add 2 tablespoons water, reduce heat, cover, and simmer for 6–7 minutes or until tender. Remove with a slotted spoon to a side dish and reserve.

3. Melt the remaining butter in a large skillet over medium heat. Add the cucumbers and toss in the butter. Add the remaining water, reduce heat, cover, and simmer for 3 minutes or until tender. Remove the cover, raise heat, and cook until all the juices have evaporated.

4. Add the carrots to the skillet. Season with salt and pepper. Stir in the crème fraîche or sour cream and reduce until thickened and sauce coats a spoon. Add the tarragon and serve at once.

V·A·R·I·A·T·I·O·N

The cucumbers and carrots are equally delicious with finely minced fresh dill or mint. Substitute 2–3 tablespoons dill or mint for the tarragon.

2 medium cucumbers or 1 large burpless cucumber, unpeeled, seeded, and cut into pieces ½ by ½ by 1 inch

Coarse salt

4 tablespoons unsalted butter

3 medium carrots, peeled, trimmed, and cut into matchsticks ½ by ½ by 1 inch

Pinch of granulated sugar

4 tablespoons water

Freshly ground black pepper

½ cup Crème Fraîche (see below) or sour cream

2–3 tablespoons finely minced fresh tarragon

SERVES 4

CRÈME FRAÎCHE

For homemade crème fraîche combine 2 cups heavy cream (not ultrapasteurized) and 2 tablespoons buttermilk in glass jar. Whisk until combined and set aside at room temperature for 24 hours. Chill until ready to use.

Sauté of Chicken Breasts in Lemon & Cucumber Sauce

5 pickling cucumbers or 1 burpless
  (about 1½ pounds)

Coarse salt

6 tablespoons unsalted butter

4 whole chicken breasts, skinned,
  boned, and cut in half

Salt and freshly ground white
  pepper

Flour for dredging

2 teaspoons corn oil

¾–1 cup Chicken Stock
  (page 37) or bouillon

½ cup heavy cream

Juice of ½ lemon

1 Beurre Manié (page 54)

GARNISH

2 tablespoons finely minced
  fresh dill or parsley

SERVES 4–5

P·R·E·P·A·R·A·T·I·O·N

1. Peel the cucumbers and cut in half lengthwise. Remove the seeds with a grapefruit spoon and cut crosswise into ¼-inch slices. Place in a colander, sprinkle with coarse salt, and let drain for 1 hour.

2. Dry the cucumbers thoroughly on paper towels. Heat 3 tablespoons butter in a large skillet. Add the cucumbers and sauté over high heat for 3–4 minutes or until lightly browned. Set aside.

3. Season the chicken breasts with salt and pepper and dredge lightly in flour, shaking off the excess.

4. Melt the remaining butter and oil in a heavy 12-inch skillet and add the chicken breasts, 3 or 4 pieces at a time. Do not crowd the pan. Sauté over high heat until nicely browned on both sides. Repeat with remaining chicken breasts and when all are browned add ½ cup of broth. Return all the breasts to the skillet, cover, and simmer for 3–4 minutes.

5. Uncover the skillet. Remove the chicken to a side dish, add the remaining stock to the skillet, bring to a boil, and reduce by half. Add the cream and lemon juice. Bring to a boil and whisk in bits of beurre manié, just enough to thicken the sauce until the point that it coats a spoon.

6. Add the cucumbers. Taste and correct the seasoning.

7. Return the chicken breasts to the skillet; spoon the sauce over and heat through. Transfer to a serving platter, sprinkle with dill or parsley, and serve immediately.

Cucumber Boats with Goat Cheese & Summer Herbs

1. In a bowl combine the goat cheese, sour cream, olive oil, and lemon juice. Mash the mixture with the back of a fork until it is smooth. Add the scallions, thyme, rosemary, and olives. Season with salt and pepper and chill until serving time.

2. Peel the cucumbers, cut them in half lengthwise, and scoop the seeds out carefully with a grapefruit spoon. Sprinkle the cucumber "boats" with coarse salt and let them drain, upside down, on paper towels for 30 minutes to 1 hour.

3. Wipe the boats dry with additional paper towels and fill with the goat cheese mixture. Place on a serving platter and sprinkle with thyme and rosemary leaves. Serve chilled with finely sliced buttered black bread.

4 tablespoons mild goat cheese, crumbled

½ cup sour cream

2 tablespoons olive oil, preferably extra-virgin

1 teaspoon lemon juice

2 tablespoons finely minced scallions

1 teaspoon fresh thyme leaves and 1 teaspoon fresh rosemary leaves, finely minced, plus more for garnish

6 black oil-cured olives, preferably Niçoise, pitted and finely minced

Salt and freshly ground black pepper

4–5 small cucumbers

Coarse salt

GARNISH

Tiny leaves of fresh thyme and rosemary

SERVES 8–10

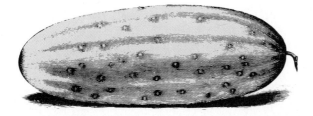

Fillets of Sole in Cucumber & Tomato Sauce

6 tablespoons unsalted butter

2 medium cucumbers, peeled, seeded, and cut crosswise into ¼-inch slices

1 cup Classic Plum Tomato Sauce (page 92)

¼ cup heavy cream

Salt and freshly ground white pepper

1½ pounds fillet of sole (about 6 small fillets)

Flour for dredging

1 teaspoon olive oil

2 tablespoons finely minced fresh dill

SERVES 6

P·R·E·P·A·R·A·T·I·O·N

1. In a large skillet melt 2 tablespoons butter over medium heat. Add the cucumber slices and sauté quickly until lightly browned. Add the tomato sauce and cream and season with salt and pepper. Keep warm.

2. Dry the fish thoroughly on paper towels. Season with salt and pepper. Dredge lightly in flour, shaking off the excess.

3. In another large skillet melt 2 tablespoons butter and the oil over medium-high heat. Add half of the fillets and sauté for 2–3 minutes on each side until lightly browned. Transfer to a warm platter and add the remaining butter to the skillet. Sauté the remaining sole fillets and transfer to the warm platter.

4. Spoon the warm sauce over the fish and sprinkle with the minced dill. Serve at once.

R·E·M·A·R·K·S

Other fish fillets (such as salmon or swordfish) can be used successfully in this same preparation. You may also make this dish with sautéed sea scallops.

Cucumber, Shrimp & Mushroom Salad in Mustard Dill Mayonnaise

1. Place the cucumber in a colander, sprinkle with salt, and let drain for 30 minutes.

2. While the cucumbers are draining, *marinate the mushrooms and shrimp:* In a medium mixing bowl combine the oil, 2 tablespoons vinegar, and the mustard. Whisk until well blended. Add the diced shrimp and mushrooms and marinate for 30 minutes.

3. In a salad bowl combine the remaining vinegar, mayonnaise, and minced dill. Season with salt and pepper and set aside.

4. Dry the salted cucumbers on a double layer of paper towels. Drain the shrimp and mushrooms well and add them, together with the cucumbers, to the salad bowl. Toss gently with the mayonnaise. Taste and correct seasoning. Cover and chill for 2–4 hours.

5. Serve slightly chilled on individual serving plates lined with lettuce leaves and garnish each with a sprig of fresh dill.

1 pound cucumbers (about 1 burpless or 4 pickling), peeled, seeded, and cut into ½-inch cubes

Salt

6 tablespoons olive oil

2 tablespoons plus 1 teaspoon red wine vinegar

1 tablespoon Dijon mustard

1 pound medium shrimp, cooked, peeled, and diced

½ pound fresh mushrooms, wiped, trimmed, and diced

¾ cup Homemade Mayonnaise (page 13)

3 tablespoons finely minced fresh dill

Freshly ground black pepper

GARNISH

Small leaves of garden lettuce
Sprigs of fresh dill

SERVES 6

BURPEE'S

PEPPERS

Christopher Columbus discovered peppers in the gardens of Caribbean Indians, and within years they were being grown throughout Europe. Today, you can venture into an open-air market almost anywhere in the world and be dazzled by heaps of glistening peppers in shades of green, red, purple, and yellow. Italians love their peppers almost to the point of reverence and work them into the most glorious displays. Raw, the colorful vegetable may be arranged as an artistic centerpiece to the antipasti table: a platter of roasted peppers with an accompaniment of sliced fresh mozzarella, anchovies, and black olives or with just a splash of fruity olive oil is resplendent, simple, yet irresistible. In Hungary and the Balkan countries, peppers are a staple that has inspired such magnificent regional dishes as chicken paprikash, marinated lamb and pepper kebab, and spicy stuffed pepper soups.

Mexican cuisine as we know it today simply would not exist without the fiery peppers collectively known as chilies. Myriad varieties are grown, each with its own special qualities and uses that help make the creative cookery of Mexico so distinctive. And in India, where incendiary fare is a way of life, plantings of both hot and sweet peppers became so widespread that early botanists incorrectly believed the plants to be indigenous.

Sweet peppers have always been popular in the United States and are a must in every vegetable garden. In the past few years many more varieties of peppers have become available to the home cook. Now you can find red, yellow, and green frying peppers in many markets along with various types of hot chili peppers both green and red. The new, innovative American cuisine that has been greatly influenced by fine, creative chefs in California and the Southwest demonstrates just how exciting and versatile this vegetable can be.

I always add one-half cup of finely diced green peppers to tuna, egg, rice, and potato salads; I also love them in a Greek salad, combined with tomatoes, cucumbers, radishes, and onions. I rarely use green peppers in tossed salads, as they tend to domi-

nate the subtle tastes typical of salad greens, but red peppers, which are fully ripened green peppers, are less assertive and can supply tossed salads with welcome color without overwhelming other ingredients. Their delicate sweetness also makes red peppers delicious when quartered raw and served with a zesty dip, stewed in olive oil and butter, or stuffed with rice or a savory meat filling.

When roasted, green peppers acquire a mellow, smoky taste that imparts a new dimension to many dishes. One of my favorite ways to serve roasted peppers is simply quartered and seeded. With the charred skins left on, I place them in a decorative pattern on a round serving platter, dribble them with olive oil, and add freshly snipped thyme leaves and crumbled young goat cheese. A generous grinding of black pepper and a few oil-cured black olives complete this effortless summer appetizer. Roasted red peppers are perhaps even more interesting and versatile than the green because of their unimposing good flavor. Late in summer, when both green and red peppers grace the garden, I like to use them together to create unique taste sensations in pastas, ragouts, and with other roasted vegetables such as eggplant and tomatoes.

S·T·O·R·A·G·E

Whole peppers can be kept refrigerated in plastic or brown paper bags but do best when refrigerated in the vegetable bin where they will keep up to two weeks. Red peppers have a much shorter storage life than the green because they are already completely ripened and therefore more delicate. However, even peppers that have started to shrivel or show damp spots can still be used successfully in stews and soups. Once sliced, peppers will not keep for more than a day or two. Roasted, peeled, and seeded peppers store well in a jar, covered over with about one-quarter inch of olive oil and refrigerated. If you have surplus red peppers at the end of the season, your best bet is to pickle them for winter use—they make marvelous Christmas gifts.

Freezing peppers changes their texture and renders them

limp, but they do retain their flavor and can be used successfully in stews and soups. Core and seed the peppers, cube or slice them, and freeze in freezer bags or freezer containers.

To dry hot peppers, wait until they turn red and then string them together loosely by pushing heavy thread through their stems. Hang in a cool, airy spot out of the sun.

G·A·R·D·E·N·I·N·G

I have no trouble growing peppers, but seeds must be started indoors about two months before the last danger of spring frost. In short-season areas, choose fast-maturing varieties so your plants will have enough time to ripen the fruits before fall frosts.

Consider your favorite ways of using peppers and select the varieties best suited for the purpose. Use sweet bell peppers mostly for slicing and dicing in salads, and for stuffing. If you entertain often and enjoy setting a colorful table, grow a few plants of a purple variety along with those that mature to red or yellow. The long, narrow varieties like Sweet Banana or the incredibly productive Gypsy Hybrid are best for frying and sautées. Hot peppers are available in degrees of pungency ranging from very mild (Zippy Hybrid) to hot (jalapeño and serrano) to fiery (cayenne).

I plant at least two varieties of sweet bell pepper, a long, sweet Italian-style pepper (usually Sweet Banana) and two hot peppers, which I dry at the end of the season. I also try to include some cherry peppers because the small, round fruit is my favorite for pickling. The plants are so ornamental that, if I run out of room in the vegetable garden, I tuck a couple in a flower bed.

Don't be tempted to set pepper plants out too early in spring. At best, plants will merely be inactive when night temperatures fall below 55°F; more likely, they will turn yellow and become stunted. Overfertilizing of peppers results in lush foliage but little fruit. I use Burpee fertilizer at planting time. Dry soil may cause blossom drop, as may excessively high temperatures or low humidity. Flowering generally will resume as weather conditions become more favorable.

ROASTED RED OR GREEN PEPPERS

Peppers can be roasted both indoors and outdoors. When roasting indoors, place over a medium-high gas flame or directly on electric coils until blackened and charred on all sides. For outdoors, peppers should be placed directly over hot coals. Wrap peppers in damp paper towels until cool enough to handle. To peel, run peppers under cold water and remove all skin. Core and seed. Note: When working with hot peppers, wash hands thoroughly afterward or wear rubber gloves.

H·A·R·V·E·S·T·I·N·G

Use pruning shears or a sharp knife to cut peppers from the plant. Twisting by hand may cause the rather brittle branches to bend and break.

BURPEE'S RUBY KING.

R·E·C·I·P·E·S

Pepper, Onion & Anchovy Pizza 67

Fettuccine with Seafood in Pepper Sauce 68

Basque Tomato & Pepper Soup 69

Hearty Viennese Pepper & Beef Soup 70

Balkan Grilled Pepper Salad 71

Mediterranean Stuffed Peppers 72

Mary's Pickled Hot Peppers 73

Tiny Boulettes with Rigatoni & Peppers 74

Spicy Sauté of Peppers & Sausages 76

Pepper, Zucchini & Potato Frittata 77

Pepper, Onion & Anchovy Pizza

P·R·E·P·A·R·A·T·I·O·N

1. In a heavy skillet heat 4 tablespoons olive oil over medium-high heat. Add the red onions and cook for 5 minutes, stirring constantly. Add the thyme and season with salt and pepper. Cover, reduce heat, and cook for 30–35 minutes or until soft and lightly browned. Set aside.

2. Preheat oven to 425°F. Brush a 12-inch black pizza pan lightly with oil and sprinkle with cornmeal. Set aside.

3. Roll out the pizza dough on a lightly floured surface into a 9-inch circle. Transfer the dough to the prepared pizza pan and stretch gently from the center outwards to the edge of pan. If the dough becomes too elastic, let rest for 5 minutes and begin again.

4. Spread the onion jam evenly over the surface of the dough, leaving a ½-inch border. Top with red peppers and anchovy fillets. Sprinkle with oregano, a good grinding of pepper, and the remaining 2 teaspoons olive oil. Place in the center of the preheated oven and bake for 12–18 minutes or until pizza is bubbly and crust is crisp and nicely browned. Remove from the oven and serve at once cut into wedges.

4 tablespoons plus 2 teaspoons olive oil

4 medium red onions, peeled, halved, and thinly sliced

1 tablespoon fresh thyme

Salt and freshly ground black pepper

Coarse yellow cornmeal for sprinkling on pizza pan

½ recipe Pizza Dough (see below)

2 large red bell peppers, roasted, peeled (page 65), and thinly sliced

4 anchovy fillets, cut in half lengthwise

½ tablespoon fresh oregano

SERVES 4

PIZZA DOUGH

In a small bowl combine ¼ cup warm water, 1 teaspoon dry yeast, and ½ teaspoon sugar. Set aside for 10 minutes. Combine 2¾ cups all-purpose flour and 1½ teaspoons salt in food processor. With machine running, add yeast mixture and ¾ cup cold water mixed with 3 tablespoons olive oil in a steady stream. Process 1 minute. Dough will be soft and sticky. Knead dough by hand 30 seconds, divide in half, place in plastic bags, and refrigerate 30 minutes. Dough is ready to be used. Makes two 12-inch pizzas.

Fettuccine with Seafood in Pepper Sauce

6 tablespoons olive oil, preferably
   extra-virgin

2 tablespoons finely minced fresh
   shallots

3 medium cloves garlic, peeled and
   finely minced

3 medium green bell peppers and 3
   medium red bell peppers, cored,
   seeded, and cut into ½-inch
   cubes

5 large ripe tomatoes, peeled,
   seeded, and chopped

2 teaspoons fresh thyme

2 teaspoons fresh oregano

Salt and freshly ground black
   pepper

1 large red pepper, cored, seeded,
   and cut into a fine julienne

1 pound fresh fettuccine

½ pound medium shrimp, peeled

½ pound small bay scallops

2 tablespoons unsalted butter

GARNISH

2–3 tablespoons finely minced fresh
   parsley

ACCOMPANIMENT

Bowl of freshly grated Parmesan
   cheese

SERVES 6

P·R·E·P·A·R·A·T·I·O·N

1. In a 4-quart casserole heat 3 tablespoons oil over medium heat. Add the shallots and 1 minced clove of garlic. Cook until soft but not browned.

2. Add the cubed green and red peppers, tomatoes, thyme, oregano, salt, and pepper. Bring to a boil, reduce heat, cover, and simmer for 1 hour 30 minutes.

3. Set a colander or sieve over a stainless steel bowl. Add the sauce, pressing down gently on the vegetables to extract all their juices. Reserve the strained sauce and 1 cup of the vegetables separately.

4. Place the reserved vegetables in a food processor or blender and process until very smooth. Transfer puree to a 3-quart saucepan together with the reserved strained sauce and whisk until well blended.

5. Place the pan over medium heat. Bring to a boil and add the red pepper julienne. Reduce heat, cover, and simmer for 10–15 minutes, stirring often to prevent sauce from sticking. Taste and correct the seasoning. Set aside.

6. Bring salted water to a boil in a large pot. Add the fettuccine and cook until just tender (al dente). Do not overcook. Immediately add 2 cups cold water to the pot to stop further cooking. Drain the pasta thoroughly and set aside.

7. Dry the scallops on paper towels.

8. In a heavy 12-inch skillet, heat the remaining olive oil and butter over medium-high heat. When hot, add the shrimp and cook, stirring constantly, for 1 minute. Remove with a slotted spoon to a side dish. Add the scallops and sauté for 1 minute. Return the shrimp to the skillet. Add the parsley, remaining garlic, salt, and pepper. Add the tomato/pepper sauce and cook 30 seconds to 1 minute more, until seafood is just done. Do not overcook. Taste and correct the seasoning.

9. Add the pasta to the skillet and toss in the hot sauce to just heat through. Sprinkle with the minced parsley and serve directly from the skillet with a bowl of Parmesan cheese and French bread.

Basque Tomato & Pepper Soup

P·R·E·P·A·R·A·T·I·O·N

1. Heat the oil over medium heat in a large casserole. Add the carrots and onions, reduce heat, cover, and cook 8–10 minutes or until barely tender. Add the stock, tomatoes, and peppers and simmer for 10 minutes. Add the zucchini and simmer 10 minutes more or until just tender. Season the soup with salt, pepper, and a pinch of cayenne.

2. Just before serving, whisk in the sour cream. Do not let the mixture come to a boil. Garnish with fresh coriander leaves. Serve hot.

3 tablespoons olive oil

2 small carrots, trimmed, peeled, and thinly sliced

2 medium onions, peeled, cut in half, and thinly sliced

5 cups Chicken Stock (page 37) or bouillon

4 large ripe tomatoes, peeled, seeded, and quartered

2 large red bell peppers, cored, seeded, and finely diced

2 small zucchini, trimmed and finely diced

Salt and freshly ground black pepper

Pinch of cayenne pepper

½–¾ cup sour cream

GARNISH

2 tablespoons fresh coriander (cilantro) leaves

SERVES 4–6

Hearty Viennese Pepper & Beef Soup

3 tablespoons unsalted butter

2 teaspoons peanut oil

2 medium onions, peeled and finely minced

1 teaspoon finely minced garlic

2 small fresh or dried cayenne peppers

2 pounds beef chuck, trimmed, cut into ¾-inch cubes

Salt and freshly ground black pepper

3 large green bell peppers, cored, seeded, and thinly sliced

1 tablespoon imported paprika

1 tablespoon caraway seeds

4 large ripe tomatoes, peeled, seeded, and pureed

8 cups beef bouillon

1 pound new potatoes, peeled and diced

GARNISH

Bowl of sour cream

SERVES 6

P·R·E·P·A·R·A·T·I·O·N

1. In a large casserole heat the butter and oil over medium heat. Add the onions, garlic, and cayenne peppers and cook until soft but not browned.

2. Add the beef cubes, stirring constantly, until the beef begins to brown. Season with salt and pepper. Add the green peppers, paprika, and caraway seeds and cook for 5 minutes.

3. Add the tomatoes and bouillon, bring to a boil, reduce heat, and simmer covered for about 2 hours or until the meat is just tender.

4. Add the potatoes and continue cooking until the potatoes are tender. Taste and correct the seasoning and serve in deep bowls topped with spoonfuls of sour cream and accompanied by black bread and a bowl of sweet butter.

Balkan Grilled Pepper Salad

P·R·E·P·A·R·A·T·I·O·N

1. In a serving bowl combine the oil, vinegar, garlic, salt, and pepper. Add the onion, peppers, tomatoes, olives, and oregano leaves. Toss well. Cover and marinate for 1–2 hours at room temperature.

2. Just before serving, taste and correct the seasoning and transfer to a shallow serving dish. Sprinkle with the feta and serve with a crusty loaf of bread.

4 tablespoons olive oil, preferably extra-virgin

1–2 tablespoons red wine vinegar

1 large clove garlic, peeled and mashed

Salt and freshly ground black pepper

1 small red onion, peeled, quartered, and thinly sliced

2 large green bell peppers and 2 large red bell peppers, roasted, peeled (page 65), cut into ½-inch-wide strips

10 ripe cherry tomatoes, cut in half

10 small black oil-cured olives, preferably Greek, pitted and cut in half

1 tablespoon fresh oregano leaves

GARNISH

⅔ cup feta cheese, crumbled

SERVES 6

Mediterranean Stuffed Peppers

1 recipe Basque Vegetable Paella
 (page 99)

3–4 tablespoons fresh coriander
 (cilantro)

½ teaspoon ground cumin

Salt and freshly ground black
 pepper

10–12 medium green bell peppers
 or ½ green and ½ red

4 tablespoons olive oil

½–¾ cup water

GARNISH

1 tablespoon olive oil, preferably
 extra-virgin

1 tablespoon red wine vinegar,
 preferably sherry

Finely minced fresh parsley

SERVES 10–12

P·R·E·P·A·R·A·T·I·O·N

1. Preheat oven to 375°F.

2. In a large bowl combine the paella with the fresh coriander and ground cumin. Correct the seasoning and toss well.

3. Cut the tops off the peppers and remove the white membranes and seeds. Fill the peppers loosely with the rice stuffing. Stand the peppers in a shallow baking dish. Dribble with the olive oil and add ½ cup water to the baking dish. Place in the center of the preheated oven and bake for 1 hour 15 minutes to 1 hour 30 minutes, basting with the pan juices every 10 to 15 minutes. Add the remaining water if juices run dry.

5. When the peppers are done, remove them from the oven and let cool. Slice the peppers in half vertically. Place the peppers, stuffing side up, onto a large serving platter. Dribble with the oil and vinegar. Sprinkle with a good grinding of black pepper and minced parsley. Serve at room temperature.

R·E·M·A·R·K·S

The peppers are even better when prepared a day in advance. Refrigerate overnight and then bring back to room temperature before serving. You may also serve the peppers warm.

Mary's Pickled Hot Peppers

These quickly prepared hot peppers make a delicious side dish to barbecued meats, chicken, or a simple hamburger. I often dice one or two of these and add them to a summer potato or tuna salad.

P·R·E·P·A·R·A·T·I·O·N

1. Place the sliced peppers in a large bowl and set aside.

2. In a medium saucepan bring vinegar to a simmer. Pour over the peppers and let stand for 25 minutes. Drain and discard vinegar.

3. Add the oregano, garlic, salt, and 4 cups oil to the bowl. Toss and transfer the peppers with a slotted spoon to 4 perfectly clean pint jars, leaving a ½-inch headspace. Pack down firmly. Pour the oil over the peppers, leaving a ¼-inch headspace. Let the jars sit at room temperature, uncovered, overnight.

4. The next day, if the oil has settled so that the peppers are exposed, fill the jars with a little more oil to cover the peppers completely. Seal tightly and store in a cool place for 3–4 months before opening.

R·E·M·A·R·K·S

There is no need to boil the jars of peppers in a water bath since the peppers are completely immersed in oil.

2 pounds hot cherry peppers, both red and green, stemmed and cut crosswise into ¼-inch slices with seeds

5 cups white vinegar

2 tablespoons fresh oregano leaves

4 medium cloves garlic, peeled and thinly sliced

Salt to taste

4–5 cups oil (a combination of ½ olive oil and ½ corn oil)

MAKES 4 PINTS

Tiny Boulettes with Rigatoni & Peppers

1½ pounds ground chuck or a
  mixture of beef and pork

2 tablespoons finely minced fresh
  parsley

1 large egg, lightly beaten

2 teaspoons fresh marjoram leaves

Salt and freshly ground black
  pepper

¼ teaspoon imported paprika

2 teaspoons fresh thyme leaves

4 cloves garlic, peeled and finely
  minced

2 tablespoons unsalted butter

3 medium onions, peeled and finely
  minced

3 tablespoons water

½ cup bread crumbs, soaked in
  milk and drained

All-purpose flour for dredging

6–8 tablespoons olive oil

¾ cup dry white wine

2 large green bell peppers and 2
  large red bell peppers, cored,
  seeded, and thinly sliced

4 large ripe tomatoes, peeled,
  seeded, and chopped

1 Bouquet Garni (page 100)

1 cup beef bouillon

¾ pound rigatoni

½ cup freshly grated Parmesan
  cheese

SERVES 6

P·R·E·P·A·R·A·T·I·O·N

1. *The boulettes:* In a mixing bowl combine the ground meat, parsley, egg, marjoram, salt, pepper, paprika, thyme, and 2 cloves garlic, minced. Work the mixture until it is well blended. Set aside.

2. Heat the butter in a small heavy skillet. Add 1 minced onion and cook over medium heat until soft but not browned. Add to the meat mixture with the water and bread crumbs. Work the mixture again and season with salt and pepper. Form the meat mixture into small balls about the size of a quarter. Dredge them lightly in flour on all sides.

3. Preheat oven to 350°F.

4. In a large heavy skillet, heat 2 tablespoons oil over medium heat. Add the meat balls a few at a time, without crowding the pan, and sauté on all sides until nicely browned. Transfer the meat balls with a slotted spoon to a heavy casserole.

5. Continue sautéeing the remaining *boulettes*, adding more oil as necessary. Transfer to the casserole and season all the browned meat balls with salt and pepper and set aside.

6. Add the remaining oil to the skillet. Add the remaining onions and garlic and cook, scraping the bottom of the pan well, until the mixture is nicely browned. Do not burn. Add the wine, bring to a boil, and reduce to ¼ cup. Add the green and red peppers and tomatoes. Season with salt and pepper.

7. Bring the tomato/pepper mixture to a boil, then add it to the casserole. Bury the bouquet garni in the casserole and add the bouillon.

8. Cover the casserole tightly and place in the center of the pre-heated oven. Braise for 1 hour 30 minutes, basting several times with the pan juices.

9. When the meat balls are done, remove from the oven and degrease the pan juices carefully. Cover and keep warm.

10. Bring plenty of lightly salted water to a boil. Add the rigatoni and cook until just tender. Drain thoroughly and toss with the meat ball ragout and half of the Parmesan cheese. Taste and correct the seasoning. Sprinkle with remaining Parmesan and serve hot directly from the casserole.

Spicy Sauté of Peppers & Sausages

2 tablespoons olive oil, preferably
  extra-virgin

1 pound sweet Italian sausage

1 small fresh cayenne pepper or 1
  dry red chili pepper, broken

1 large onion, peeled and finely
  minced

2 large cloves garlic, peeled and
  finely minced

4 large ripe tomatoes, peeled,
  seeded, and chopped

1 teaspoon tomato paste

2 medium green bell peppers and 2
  medium red bell peppers, cored,
  seeded, and finely sliced

1 tablespoon fresh oregano

2 large fresh basil leaves

Optional: 8 sun-dried tomato
  halves, finely diced

Salt and freshly ground black
  pepper

3 ounces prosciutto, trimmed of all
  fat, finely diced

GARNISH

1 cup freshly grated Parmesan
  cheese

SERVES 4–5

P·R·E·P·A·R·A·T·I·O·N

1. In a large heavy skillet heat the olive oil over medium heat. Add the sausage and cook until nicely browned on all sides. Remove the sausage to a cutting surface. Cut crosswise into ¼-inch slices and set aside.

2. Discard all but 3 tablespoons fat from the skillet. Add the cayenne or chili pepper, onion, and garlic. Cook until soft and nicely browned.

3. Add the tomatoes, tomato paste, green and red peppers, oregano, basil leaves, optional sun-dried tomatoes, and season with salt and pepper. Cover and simmer for 20–25 minutes, stirring often, until the juices have reduced and the sauce has thickened.

4. Add the sliced sausage and prosciutto and simmer for another 5 minutes. Taste and correct the seasoning. Sprinkle with Parmesan and serve at once with a loaf of crusty Italian bread.

V·A·R·I·A·T·I·O·N·S

1. Serve accompanied by Corn-Studded Polenta (page 43). Spoon the polenta into 6 individual deep serving bowls and top each with some of the peppers and sausages. Sprinkle with Parmesan and serve at once.

2. The peppers and sausages may be tossed with ¾ pound cooked pasta and heated through. Serve accompanied by a bowl of freshly grated Parmesan and a loaf of crusty French bread.

Pepper, Zucchini & Potato Frittata

P·R·E·P·A·R·A·T·I·O·N

1. Preheat oven to 350°F.

2. Whisk the eggs thoroughly in a large bowl. Season with salt, pepper, and a dash of Tabasco. Set aside.

3. In a 10-inch skillet, melt 2 tablespoons butter over medium heat. Add the ham and sauté until lightly browned. Remove with a slotted spoon to a side dish and reserve.

4. Discard all but 1 tablespoon fat from the skillet. Add 2 tablespoons olive oil and when hot add the onion and garlic and cook, stirring constantly, until soft and lightly browned.

5. Add the green peppers and zucchini, season with salt and pepper, reduce heat, cover, and cook for 8–10 minutes or until the vegetables are just tender.

6. Add the potatoes and ham and just heat through.

7. Pour the egg mixture into the skillet and cook for 2–3 minutes or until the bottom is set and lightly browned.

8. Sprinkle with the Parmesan and place in the center of the preheated oven. Bake for 10–12 minutes or until the eggs are just set and lightly browned.

9. Serve right from the pan, cut into wedges.

8 large eggs
Salt and freshly ground black pepper
Dash of Tabasco sauce
2 tablespoons unsalted butter
½ cup finely diced lean smoked ham
2 tablespoons olive oil
1 medium onion, peeled, halved, and thinly sliced
2 medium cloves garlic, peeled and crushed
2 medium green bell peppers, cored, seeded, and cut into ½-inch squares
2 small zucchini, trimmed and cut into ½-inch cubes
2 medium new potatoes, cooked, peeled, and cut into ½-inch cubes
2–3 tablespoons freshly grated Parmesan cheese

SERVES 6

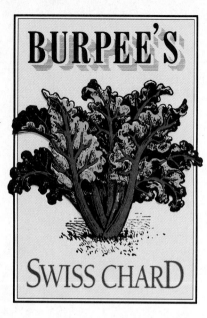

BURPEE'S

SWISS CHARD

While I was growing up, Swiss chard was always plentiful in our garden. The plants can stand dry weather very well, which is no doubt one reason for its popularity in Mediterranean countries. Although it is difficult to find many recipes in older regional cookbooks, in Europe there are certain classic preparations for which chard is a must. In southern France chard is used for a unique sweet tart topped with apricot preserves (page 84). Italians use chard in stuffings for veal rolls as well as for a braised shoulder of veal. In Venice a delicious chard cream sauce is classically served as an accompaniment to homemade potato dumplings.

Surprisingly few American gardeners have caught on to the delights of growing and cooking with chard. Yet chard is not particular about soil or climate, suffers little damage from heat, insects, or disease, and can be harvested continually for four or five months—throughout summer and fall—in most parts of the country. On the nutritional scale, chard is one of the most valuable vegetables in the garden, nearly bursting with vitamins A and C (like all dark leafy greens), plus iron and other minerals. While growing, chard's crinkled, deep green foliage is so attractive that I sometimes plant this nearly indestructible green as an edging for the vegetable garden. Since chard is an extremely prolific plant, and virtually carefree, it is an easy and rewarding addition to even the smallest vegetable garden.

Sometimes called leaf beet, leaf chard, sea kale, or spinach beet, chard is grown not only for its large, spinachlike leaves, but for its mild-tasting white ribs. Indeed, chard is two delicious vegetables in one. Garden-fresh chard is a far cry from the market vegetable, whose leaves are very large and often limp, wilted, and tough. By growing your own, you can pick smaller leaves that will be tender and not stringy.

Although chard cannot be eaten raw, it can be cooked in many simple and quick ways suitable for the summer kitchen. The green leaves taste somewhat like earthy spinach and can be cooked in any way suitable for spinach. After removing them from

the ribs, I often sauté the leaves in a little olive oil with a sliced garlic clove or two, and then garnish with sautéed pine nuts and some toasted sesame seeds. Other times I steam the leaves and combine them with diced fresh goat cheese, a sprinkling of herbs, and a light custard. Baked and served hot, this delicious flan makes a wonderful accompaniment to all meats and fish.

The broad ribs have a crisp, beetlike flavor and are deliciously crunchy. Because the ribs take longer to cook than the leaves, the two parts of the vegetable are always cooked separately and then combined. This makes for an interesting contrast of color and texture. I find that the ribs are best prepared simply. Cut them into one- to one-and-a-half-inch pieces, blanch quickly, and then simmer with a touch of butter and cream. The diced ribs are an excellent addition to a summer minestrone (page 97). They can also be blanched and then sautéed together with cooked and diced beets. Although Swiss chard does not lend itself to being used raw in salads, the slightly steamed ribs are a delicious, and unexpected, addition to the salad bowl.

S·T·O·R·A·G·E

Swiss chard is one of the few vegetables that can be picked as needed, or ignored for many days without quickly spoiling or growing overmature, so you can pick the leaves as you need them. However, if you must store chard it is best to leave it unwashed and kept in a plastic bag; it will keep refrigerated for three to five days. If you plan to keep chard for a longer period of time, I suggest you freeze it. Cut the leaves away from the ribs and use the ribs right away. Wash the leaves well in several changes of lukewarm water and cook them with just the water that clings to the leaves; they will keep for a day or two in the refrigerator or can be frozen in containers. Frozen chard can be used successfully in many preparations that call for spinach.

G·A·R·D·E·N·I·N·G

Unlike greens such as spinach or lettuce, Swiss chard does not bolt to seed in hot weather. Its needs are much like those of beets, to which Swiss chard is closely related (despite its lack of a thickened root). Chard can be planted any time in spring, but I usually sow seeds early, along with my lettuce. Where winters are mild, you can sow anytime from fall to spring. During drought, water whenever the leaves show the slightest hint of wilt.

The leaves of Burpee's Fordhook Giant make the tenderest greens of any Swiss chard. Also quite good is Burpee's Rhubarb Chard. Its stalks are colored a vibrant crimson, as are the veins of the lush foliage, making this variety among the most picturesque of all vegetables.

H·A·R·V·E·S·T·I·N·G

Picking generally begins two months after sowing, when outer foliage is about eight inches high. I use a sharp knife to slice the stalks of the outer leaves, allowing the inner foliage to continue growing. This way, fresh leaves can be harvested every few days. You can also harvest an entire plant at once; if an inch or two of the plant's crown is left above ground, new foliage will soon appear. Swiss chard can be cut back like this a few times during the summer and well into autumn. The final harvest will not be damaged by an early snowfall.

R·E·C·I·P·E·S

Creamy Swiss Chard & Leek Soup 82

Sauté of Swiss Chard with Ginger & Garlic 83

Sweet Swiss Chard Tart Provençale 84

Baked Swiss Chard Leaves with Vegetable Paella 85

BASIC TART SHELL

In a food processor bowl, combine 2 cups all-purpose flour, ½ teaspoon salt, and 12 tablespoons unsalted butter, cut into 9 pieces and chilled. Pulse quickly until the mixture resembles oatmeal. Add 3 tablespoons of ice water and pulse quickly until the mixture begins to come together.

By hand, form into a ball, then flatten into a disc, wrap in plastic, and refrigerate for 30 to 40 minutes. Roll into a circle about ⅛ inch thick. Place into the tart pan, trim excess dough, and crimp edges. Prick the bottom of the shell with a fork and chill for 30 minutes.

Preheat the oven to 425°. Line shell with parchment paper, fill with dried beans, and place on a cookie sheet. Place in the center of the oven for 12 minutes. Remove paper and beans and continue to bake for 6 to 8 minutes until dough is set. Place the pan on a wire rack to cool until needed. The tart shell at this point is partially baked.

This recipe is enough for two 9-inch tart pans or one 10-inch quiche dish, with a little bit left over.

Creamy Swiss Chard & Leek Soup

P·R·E·P·A·R·A·T·I·O·N

1½ pounds Swiss chard, well
    rinsed

5 tablespoons unsalted butter

2 medium leeks, trimmed of all but
    2 inches of greens, well rinsed
    and thinly sliced

Salt and freshly ground white
    pepper

5 cups Chicken Stock (page 37) or
    bouillon

2 tablespoons all-purpose flour

½ cup heavy cream

1 medium all-purpose potato,
    peeled and diced

1 large carrot, trimmed, peeled,
    and diced

GARNISH

2 tablespoons finely minced fresh
    chives

Optional: *Freshly grated Parmesan
    cheese*

SERVES 6

1. Separate the leaves from the stalks of the Swiss chard with a sharp knife. Dice the stalks; set aside.

2. In a large casserole melt 2 tablespoons butter, add the leeks, and season with salt and pepper. Add 3 tablespoons chicken stock, cover, and "stew" the leeks until tender.

3. Add the remaining chicken stock, bring to a boil, and add the chard leaves. Cook until wilted, cover, and simmer for 20–25 minutes, until the leaves are tender.

4. Cool the soup, transfer to a food processor or blender, and puree until smooth.

5. Melt the remaining butter in the casserole, add the flour, and cook for 1 minute without browning. Add the pureed soup, bring to a boil, and whisk in the cream. Add the diced potatoes, carrots, and chard stalks. Simmer uncovered for 20 minutes or until vegetables are tender. Taste and correct seasoning. Serve hot sprinkled with chives and optional Parmesan cheese.

Sauté of Swiss Chard with Ginger & Garlic

1. Remove the leaves from the Swiss chard, rinse thoroughly, and set aside. You should have about 2 pounds of leaves; reserve the stalks for another use.

2. Bring water to a boil in a vegetable steamer. Add ¼–⅓ of the leaves to the steamer, cover, and steam until just wilted, about 3–4 minutes. Remove and repeat with the remaining leaves. Cool enough to handle, then gently squeeze the leaves to remove the excess moisture; cut the leaves into 1-inch pieces. Set aside.

3. In a small bowl combine the soy, sherry, sugar, and cornstarch and mix thoroughly. Set the sauce aside.

4. Add the bacon to a large cold skillet and place over medium heat. Cook until lightly browned; remove with a slotted spoon and reserve.

5. Discard all but 3 tablespoons fat from the skillet, add the peanut oil, and when hot add the garlic and ginger. Immediately add the Swiss chard and quickly sauté until just heated through. Restir the sauce and add it together with the reserved bacon and cook for a few seconds longer. Taste and correct the seasoning, adding a large grinding of pepper, and serve hot.

4 pounds Swiss chard
2 tablespoons thin soy sauce
3 teaspoons dry sherry
½ teaspoon granulated sugar
1 teaspoon cornstarch
3 slices lean meaty bacon, cut into ¼-inch pieces
3 tablespoons peanut oil
2 teaspoons finely minced garlic
2 teaspoons finely minced ginger
Large grinding of black pepper

SERVES 4–6

Sweet Swiss Chard Tart Provençale

THE TART SHELL

1 cup all-purpose flour

1½ tablespoons confectioners'
    sugar

6 tablespoons cold unsalted butter,
    cut into 6 pieces

2 teaspoons egg yolk

1 tablespoon ice water

1 teaspoon freshly squeezed lemon
    juice

THE FILLING

½ pound Swiss chard leaves, well
    washed

⅓ cup granulated sugar

1 large egg

2 large egg yolks

1 cup heavy cream

1 teaspoon vanilla extract

2 teaspoons grated lemon rind

½ cup golden raisins, plumped in
    warm water for 10 minutes and
    then drained

THE GLAZE

½ cup apricot preserves

1 teaspoon grated lemon rind

1 teaspoon freshly squeezed lemon
    juice

2 tablespoons apricot brandy

SERVES 6–8

P·R·E·P·A·R·A·T·I·O·N

1. Preheat the oven to 350°F.

2. Start by making *the tart shell:* In the work bowl of a food processor, combine the flour, sugar, and butter. Process until the mixture resembles oatmeal. Add the egg yolk, ice water, and lemon juice, pulse on and off twice, then transfer to a large mixing bowl. Gather the dough and form a ball. Do not overwork.

3. Wrap the dough in foil and refrigerate 1 hour.

4. While the dough is resting, *prepare the Swiss chard leaves:* Bring plenty of water to a boil in a large saucepan. Add the chard leaves and cook for 3–4 minutes or until tender. Drain. When cool, squeeze the chard leaves with your hands to remove all liquid. Finely chop and set aside.

5. Roll out the dough. Place into a 9-inch tart pan with a removable bottom and prebake as explained for Basic Tart Shell (page 81).

6. In a large mixing bowl combine the sugar, eggs, and egg yolks, and whisk until well blended. Add the cream, vanilla, lemon rind, raisins, and chopped Swiss chard leaves and whisk until well blended. Pour the custard into the prebaked tart shell, dispersing the raisins evenly throughout.

7. Place the tart in the center of the preheated oven and bake for 25–30 minutes or until the custard is set; a toothpick when inserted should come out clean. Remove from the oven and cool completely.

8. *The glaze:* Combine preserves, lemon rind, lemon juice, and apricot brandy in a small saucepan and place over medium heat. Stir constantly until the preserves have melted; strain and spoon glaze over tart. Cut into wedges and serve slightly chilled.

Baked Swiss Chard Leaves with Vegetable Paella

P·R·E·P·A·R·A·T·I·O·N

1. Preheat the oven to 350°F.

2. In a medium bowl combine the vegetable paella with the cumin and set aside.

3. Bring plenty of water to a boil in a large saucepan. Add the Swiss chard leaves and blanch for 2 minutes or until barely tender. Drain thoroughly and dry on double layers of paper towels.

4. Lay the leaves flat, rib side up and vertically in front of you. Place 2–3 tablespoons filling in the center of each leaf, fold sides over onto filling and roll up, tucking in ends, to enclose filling completely.

5. Place the rolls in a heavy baking dish, seam side down. Drizzle with the olive oil and add the water to the baking dish. Sprinkle the rolls with sliced garlic, salt, and pepper. Cover with aluminum foil, place in the center of the oven, and bake for 25–30 minutes or until heated through, basting often with the pan juices.

6. Remove from the oven and serve warm as an accompaniment to grilled lamb or chicken.

R·E·M·A·R·K·S

You may also serve the rolls at room temperature drizzled with a little virgin olive oil and garnished with tiny black olives.

2 cups Basque Vegetable Paella (page 99)

½ teaspoon cumin seeds, roasted and crushed

12–16 large Swiss chard leaves

3 tablespoons olive oil

⅓ cup water

2 large cloves garlic, peeled and sliced

Coarse salt

Freshly ground black pepper

SERVES 6–8

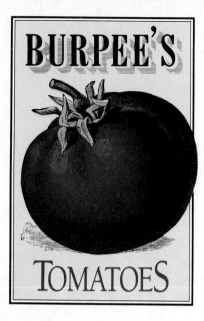

BURPEE'S

TOMATOES

O f all homegrown vegetables, tomatoes are the gardener's supreme delight. Even before I first made a commitment to have a vegetable garden, I grew tomatoes in large pots on a sunny deck. The simple yearning for the unmistakable fragrance of a vine-ripened tomato is so dear to anyone who loves this beautiful vegetable that even non-gardeners often find a way to grow two or three tomato plants.

For nine months out of the year we are faced with supermarket tomatoes that only vaguely resemble the real thing. They lack flavor, juiciness, aroma, color—you name it. Still, people buy them. Those of us with gardening convictions, and whose seasonal eating habits are strong, view these impostors with an anxious desire for those warm days of spring when we can set our own tomato plants outdoors.

Tomatoes are extremely good-natured garden specimens. The plants require plenty of sun and moisture but are otherwise undemanding. Although there are a vast number of tomato varieties to choose from, the average garden needs only about three or four plants each of an early and a main-crop variety, and two more plants if you like cherry tomatoes. If you plan to pack tomatoes and freeze some of your own tomato sauce for winter use, you should also add four or more plants of the Italian plum type.

Many recipes call for peeled and seeded tomatoes. I find the best method of peeling is to cut four or five fine incisions lengthwise into each tomato and then to drop the fruit into boiling water. In 30 seconds the peels will have separated from the flesh. Next core the fruit. To seed, cut the tomatoes in half crosswise, taking care not to squash them. You will see the seeds in their neat compartments. Scoop out the seeds with a teaspoon and season the flesh with salt, preferably coarse salt. Place the pulp in a colander to drain for 30 minutes to an hour before cooking.

Tomatoes—whole, quartered, or crushed—are among the easiest products to can, a wonderful way to store a bountiful harvest. When pressed for time, I freeze tomatoes by placing them, whole and unpeeled, in plastic bags; once defrosted, I pass

them through a tomato press. Italian plum tomatoes are best for this, and the best overall for sauce since they are more pulpy and less watery. Although I can a great quantity of sauce and freeze lots of tomatoes every fall, I still seem to run out by April.

At the very end of the season you may find yourself with some green tomatoes, both round and plum types. Aside from pickling, green tomatoes are delicious sautéed in butter enriched with a little cream and Parmesan. They can be dipped into a batter and deep-fried, or stewed together with eggplant in good olive oil with a touch of sliced garlic and a sprinkling of parsley. In North African and Middle Eastern cooking, green plum tomatoes are pickled in beet juice, which turns them a bright beet color. They look splendid packed in large jars and work beautifully as an accompaniment to boiled beef, barbecued chicken, or ribs.

More and more gardeners and chefs are experimenting not only with the popular red cherry tomatoes but with small yellow and orange varieties, which have a somewhat meatier texture and are often sweeter. Aside from lending their sweet juicy taste and lovely shape to many salads, these small tomatoes make an excellent hot vegetable. I often sauté cherry tomatoes in olive oil with a touch of garlic plus a sprinkling of fresh basil and parsley. They can also be tossed into a mixed vegetable fricassee and are delicious served as an hors d'oeuvre filled with a tuna mixture. Red, yellow, or orange varieties all work equally well in a traditional shish kebab. In the summer a mixed vegetable shish kebab of variously colored peppers, onions, eggplant, and tomatoes can be grilled along with chicken, fish, or a marinated flank steak. Sprinkled with fruity olive oil and a touch of fresh herbs, these kebabs are a lovely seasonal accompaniment to a summer barbecue.

S·T·O·R·A·G·E

It is best to keep not-quite-ripe tomatoes at room temperature. If fully mature, refrigerate them in a bowl or the vegetable bin. Do not store tomatoes in plastic bags.

Ripe tomatoes will keep refrigerated for up to ten days. For

CANNING TOMATOES

Peel and core ripe plum tomatoes. Fill hot sterilized quart-size canning jars each with 2½–3 pounds tomatoes, pressing lightly to yield juice and fill in spaces. Run spatula down side of jars to free trapped air bubbles. Add 1 teaspoon salt and large sprig fresh basil to each jar. Seal. Process in boiling water bath 45 minutes. Remove, check seals, and store in cool place. Will keep up to 1 year.

best flavor, always bring tomatoes back to room temperature before serving. When I have a surplus of ripe tomatoes, I stew them with some olive oil and minced shallots or make the Classic Plum Tomato Sauce (page 92), which keeps well for a week to ten days and freezes well.

G·A·R·D·E·N·I·N·G

Starting tomato seeds early indoors is standard gardening practice everywhere in the country, since the plants need lots of time to produce a good crop before fall frost. At outdoor planting time, the ideal transplant is no more than eight inches tall, bright green in color, and has a firm and stocky stem as well as a dense root system. If in the past your tomato seedlings turned out weak, spindly, and pale, you either did not provide sufficient light or started the seeds too early. Wait until about six weeks prior to the last expected frost before sowing tomato seeds indoors. When planting, always follow directions on seed packets since different varieties have different spacing requirements.

There are two main types of garden tomatoes: determinate and indeterminate. Determinate varieties stop growing when fruit sets on the terminal bud. The plants are generally fairly compact and bushlike, and so they're favored by some gardeners with limited space. Since they tend to ripen fruit over a shorter period, they are also chosen by many gardeners in short-season areas and those who grow tomatoes primarily for canning. Determinate varieties are best grown in cages and left unpruned, so they're also a bit easier to grow.

The most popular varieties by far—including Early Girl, Burpee's Big Girl, and Big Boy, and Burpee's Supersteak Hybrid VFN —are indeterminate. Indeterminate varieties produce vigorous vines that continue to grow and bear fruit until killed by fall frost. The plants often grow to seven or eight feet and although they can be allowed to sprawl on the ground (or, preferably, on a mulch), most people prefer to grow them trained on strong stakes or wire cages.

I've had many discussions with gardening friends about whether or not tomato plants should be pruned. According to Burpee's horticulturists, indeterminate varieties grown in cages may be left unpruned, while plants supported by stakes are best pruned to one or two main stems. This means you need to remove all side stems (called suckers) growing from the leaf nodes. There are advantages to either method. I find that the full, dense foliage of my caged plants shields the fruit from scalding midday sun, but the staking-pruning method often yields larger fruits.

When you choose tomato varieties, consider also the relative earliness. Burpee's 30-plus varieties range from Pixie Hybrid, which yields ripe tomatoes starting only 52 days from transplanting time, to the large beefsteak varieties for which you'll have to wait 80 days. If you live where the growing season is short, go for the early tomatoes.

Another hotly debated consideration is hybrid versus open-pollinated varieties. Although there are some wonderful open-pollinated varieties such as Delicious and the cherry-sized Gardener's Delight, the hybrids, by and large, are more vigorous, more disease-resistant, better adapted to a wide range of growing conditions, and yield larger crops.

In the end, I make my choice based on two criteria: how I'll use them and how they taste. Personally, I enjoy growing and serving salad tomatoes such as Early Girl Hybrid and Burpee's VF Hybrid, which bear delicious, firm, average-size fruit. For sauces and stir-fries, I prefer a plum tomato such as Roma VF, which offers a meaty texture and few seeds. And in late summer I love to pick and slice a huge, juicy, vine-ripened Supersteak fruit—a luscious meal in itself.

H·A·R·V·E·S·T·I·N·G

The very best-tasting tomato is one that is vine-ripened, picked when the entire fruit is in full blush. (Tomatoes ripen from the bottom upward.) Gently lift by hand until the fruit stem snaps. Toward the end of the season, I sometimes pick tomatoes partially ripe and then let them finish ripening indoors as a precaution against early frost. Contrary to common belief, tomatoes must never be placed to ripen in the sun. They do best in a dark, dry, cool (60°–70°F) space. Covering them with a light layer of newspaper encourages tomatoes to ripen more quickly.

R · E · C · I · P · E · S

Classic Plum Tomato Sauce 92

Tomato & Shallot Fondue 93

Pennsylvania Dutch Broiled Tomatoes 94

Cherry Tomatoes with Curry Cream Cheese Filling 94

Tomato, Dill & Rice Soup 95

Roast Leg of Lamb in Garlic & Tomato Fondue 96

Summer Minestrone 97

Basque Gazpacho 98

Basque Vegetable Paella 99

Warm Mozzarella & Beefsteak Tomato Salad 100

Ziti with Stewed Tomatoes & Steamed Mussels 101

Fricassee of Chicken with Stewed Tomatoes & Fresh Herbs 102

Grilled Tomato Salsa 103

Classic Plum Tomato Sauce

3 tablespoons olive oil, preferably
  extra-virgin
1 large onion, peeled and finely
  minced
1 stalk celery, finely minced
1 carrot, trimmed, peeled, and
  finely diced
3 tablespoons finely minced fresh
  parsley
3 large cloves garlic, peeled and
  finely minced
2 tablespoons fresh basil, chopped
1 large sprig fresh oregano
1 bay leaf
4–5 pounds ripe plum tomatoes,
  peeled, seeded, and coarsely
  chopped
2 tablespoons tomato paste
Salt and freshly ground black
  pepper

MAKES 4–5 CUPS

P·R·E·P·A·R·A·T·I·O·N

1. Heat the oil in a large heavy casserole. Add the onion, celery, carrot, parsley, garlic, and herbs and cook over low heat, partially covered, until soft but not browned.

2. Add the tomatoes and tomato paste and season with salt and pepper. Bring to a boil, reduce heat, and simmer, covered, for 1 hour 30 minutes to 2 hours, stirring several times to prevent the sauce from scorching. Taste and correct the seasoning.

3. Puree the sauce in a food processor or blender or pass it through a food mill and refrigerate in covered jars.

R·E·M·A·R·K·S

If the sauce is too thin, uncover and let it reduce to the desired consistency. The tomato sauce can be kept frozen for 2–3 months.

Tomato & Shallot Fondue

P·R·E·P·A·R·A·T·I·O·N

1. Quarter the tomatoes and place them in a large sieve over a bowl; sprinkle tomatoes with salt and drain for 4–6 hours.

2. Heat the oil in a large heavy-bottomed saucepan. Add the shallots, garlic, and bay leaf and cook the mixture over low heat for 2–3 minutes, or until soft but not browned.

3. Add the tomatoes, season with salt and pepper, add thyme, marjoram, and tomato paste, and cook over high heat for 15 minutes, stirring to prevent the mixture from scorching.

4. Reduce the heat and continue cooking for 45 minutes, or until very thick, stirring often.

5. Add the optional basil paste to the tomato fondue and correct the seasoning.

6. Transfer the fondue to a jar and store in the refrigerator until needed. The tomato fondue will keep for 2–3 weeks; it can also be frozen.

4–5 pounds fresh plum tomatoes, peeled

Salt

¼ cup olive oil, preferably extra-virgin

½ cup finely minced shallots

4 large cloves garlic, peeled and finely minced

1 bay leaf

Freshly ground black pepper

1 large sprig fresh thyme

1 teaspoon fresh marjoram

1 tablespoon tomato paste

Optional: *3–4 tablespoons Basil Paste (page 20)*

MAKES ABOUT 3 CUPS

Pennsylvania Dutch Broiled Tomatoes

6 ripe medium tomatoes

6 tablespoons dark brown sugar

6 tablespoons bread crumbs

6 tablespoons unsalted butter, cut
   into bits

SERVES 6

P·R·E·P·A·R·A·T·I·O·N

1. Preheat the broiler.

2. Cut each tomato in half horizontally and place each half cut side up on a baking sheet.

3. Sprinkle each half with ½ tablespoon sugar, ½ tablespoon bread crumbs, and ½ tablespoon butter, in that order.

4. Place the tomatoes under the broiler, 6 inches from the source of heat, and broil until the sugar caramelizes and tops are lightly browned. Serve at once.

Cherry Tomatoes with Curry Cream Cheese Filling

3 ounces cream cheese, softened

½ cup sour cream

1 tablespoon imported curry
   powder, preferably Madras

2 small dill gherkins, finely minced

3 tablespoons finely diced red onion

3 green pimiento-stuffed olives,
   finely diced

Salt and freshly ground black
   pepper

24–30 ripe cherry tomatoes

GARNISH

Leaves of Italian parsley

SERVES 8–10

P·R·E·P·A·R·A·T·I·O·N

1. In a small bowl combine the cream cheese and sour cream. Mash together until smooth with the back of a fork. Add the curry powder, gherkins, red onion, and olives. Season with salt and pepper and set aside for 1 hour to develop flavor.

2. Cut a slice off the top of each tomato opposite the stem end. Set caps aside. Scoop out the pulp very carefully with the tip of a sharp knife. Fill the tomato shells with a little of the curry/cream cheese mixture and top each with a leaf of Italian parsley and a tomato cap. Place on a round serving platter and serve at room temperature.

Tomato, Dill & Rice Soup

1. In a large heavy casserole, melt the butter over medium heat. Add the onions and cook until soft but not brown.

2. Add the thyme, marjoram, and parsley together with the crushed garlic, tomatoes, and stock. Season with salt and pepper. Bring to a boil, reduce heat, partially cover, and simmer 40–45 minutes.

3. Remove the sprigs of herbs and discard. Transfer to a food processor or blender and process until very smooth.

4. Return the soup to the casserole. Add ½ cup cooked rice and just heat through. If the soup seems too thin, add the remaining rice.

5. Just before serving, reheat the soup and whisk in the crème fraîche or sour cream and dill. Taste and correct the seasoning, adding a large grinding of pepper, and serve hot.

R·E·M·A·R·K·S

The soup can also be served slightly chilled. In this case, you may substitute yogurt for the crème fraîche or sour cream.

3 tablespoons unsalted butter

2 medium onions peeled, cut in half, and thinly sliced

1 large sprig fresh thyme

1 large sprig fresh marjoram

1 large sprig fresh parsley

1 medium clove garlic, peeled and crushed

4 large ripe tomatoes, peeled, seeded, and chopped

4 cups Chicken Stock (page 37) or bouillon

Salt and freshly ground white pepper

½–¾ cup cooked rice

½ cup Crème Fraîche (page 57) or sour cream

¼–½ cup finely minced fresh dill

SERVES 6

Roast Leg of Lamb in Garlic
& Tomato Fondue

THE LAMB

A 6–6½ pound leg of lamb

*Salt and freshly ground black
  pepper*

2 teaspoons fresh marjoram

2 teaspoons fresh thyme

2 teaspoons fresh rosemary

1½ teaspoons imported paprika

1½ teaspoons Dijon mustard

*2 large cloves garlic, peeled and
  mashed*

3 tablespoons unsalted butter

1 tablespoon olive oil

*1 medium onion, peeled and cut in
  half crosswise*

*14–16 tiny red potatoes, unpeeled
  and washed*

2 cups hot beef bouillon

THE GARLIC PUREE

1 cup beef bouillon

*1 large head garlic, separated into
  cloves and peeled*

*1¼ cup Tomato and Shallot
  Fondue (page 93)*

*Optional: 1 tablespoon cornstarch
  mixed with a little bouillon*

GARNISH

Sprigs of fresh garden cress

SERVES 6

P·R·E·P·A·R·A·T·I·O·N
---

1. Season the lamb with salt, pepper, marjoram, thyme, and rosemary. Rub the leg with paprika and mustard. Make tiny slits along the bottom of the roast and insert bits of the garlic. Set the lamb aside at room temperature for 2 hours.

2. While the lamb is marinating, *prepare the garlic puree:* In a small saucepan, bring 1 cup beef bouillon to a boil. Add the garlic cloves, reduce heat, and simmer for 45 minutes or until all the bouillon has been reduced and absorbed by the garlic cloves. Transfer the garlic to a food processor or blender and puree until smooth; add the tomato fondue and set aside.

3. Preheat the oven to 375°F.

4. In a large flameproof baking dish, heat the butter and oil. Place the onion halves, cut side down, in the dish, then add the roast and spoon some of the hot fat over it. Add the tiny potatoes around the lamb and place in the center of the oven and roast for 1 hour 20 minutes (or 12 minutes per pound for medium rare), basting it every 10 minutes with a little hot bouillon.

5. When the lamb is done, transfer to a platter together with the potatoes, cover, and keep warm.

6. Carefully degrease the pan juices and return them to the baking dish. Place baking dish over high heat and add any remaining bouillon to the pan. Bring to a boil and reduce to ½ cup. Add the tomato/garlic fondue and heat through.

7. If the sauce seems too thin, add a little of the optional cornstarch mixture, just enough to thicken the sauce. Taste and correct seasoning.

8. Thinly slice the roast and place on a serving platter. Surround with the tiny potatoes and garnish with sprigs of garden cress. Pass the sauce separately.

Summer Minestrone

P·R·E·P·A·R·A·T·I·O·N

1. In a large casserole heat the olive oil over medium-low heat. Add the onions and cook until soft but not brown.

2. Add the potatoes, carrots, celery, zucchini, diced Swiss chard stalks, tomatoes, and 4 cups chicken stock. Bring to a boil, season with salt and pepper, reduce heat, partially cover, and simmer for 35 minutes or until all the vegetables are tender.

3. Add the pasta to the soup and cook until pasta is just tender, about 6–8 minutes. Add the julienne strips of Swiss chard leaves and the basil. Cook for 2–3 minutes longer. Taste and correct the seasoning. If the soup seems too thick, add the remaining chicken stock.

4. Sprinkle the soup with 2 tablespoons of the Parmesan and serve hot directly from the casserole with the remaining Parmesan on the side.

4 tablespoons olive oil

2 medium onions, peeled, cut in half, and thinly sliced

2 medium red potatoes, peeled, cut into ½-inch cubes

2 medium carrots, peeled, cut into ½-inch cubes

2 celery stalks, diced

2 small zucchini, trimmed and diced

½ pound Swiss chard, washed, stalks diced and leaves cut into thin julienne

6 ripe medium tomatoes, peeled, seeded, and diced

4–5 cups Chicken Stock (page 37) or bouillon

Salt and freshly ground black pepper

¼ cup tiny pasta, such as tubettini or bows

½ cup fine julienne of fresh basil leaves

GARNISH

½ cup freshly grated Parmesan cheese

SERVES 6

Basque Gazpacho

Every region of Spain has its own version of this popular summer soup. Here is a flavorful and somewhat spicy gazpacho that is my favorite. You may add the traditional garnishes of minced onions, peppers, and cucumbers or serve it with a side bowl of garlic-flavored yogurt and a sprinkling of fresh cilantro.

4 thin slices day-old French bread

¼ cup olive oil

¼ cup red wine vinegar

2 medium pickling cucumbers, peeled, seeded, and diced

8 large ripe tomatoes (about 3½–4 pounds), peeled, seeded, and coarsely chopped

1 tablespoon jalapeño pepper, roasted, peeled (page 65) and finely minced

½ cup finely minced red onion

1 large clove garlic, peeled and crushed

2 cups fresh tomato juice

Optional: 1 cup Chicken Stock (page 37)

Salt and freshly ground black pepper

GARNISH

4 tablespoons finely minced fresh parsley

1 cup finely minced red onion

1 cup finely diced green bell pepper

1 cup finely diced cucumber

SERVES 6–8

P·R·E·P·A·R·A·T·I·O·N

1. Preheat oven to 250°F.

2. Cube the French bread, place on a cookie sheet, and set in the center of the preheated oven for 10 minutes. Remove and transfer to a medium mixing bowl. Add the olive oil and vinegar and toss until the bread has absorbed the dressing. Set aside.

3. In the work bowl of a food processor combine the cucumbers, tomatoes, cayenne pepper, onion, and garlic. Process the mixture until smooth.

4. Add the bread mixture to the food processor and again process until smooth.

5. Thin the mixture with the tomato juice and optional chicken stock. Season with salt and pepper and chill for at least 6 hours before serving.

6. Serve the soup chilled in individual bowls, sprinkled with minced parsley, and pass the various vegetable garnishes separately.

Basque Vegetable Paella

P·R·E·P·A·R·A·T·I·O·N

1. In a large deep heavy skillet, heat the olive oil over medium-high heat. Add the cayenne or chili pepper, onion, and bell peppers, reduce heat, and cook for 20 minutes or until vegetables are tender and onion is lightly browned.

2. Add the garlic, paprika, thyme, zucchini, and tomatoes. Season with salt and pepper. Cover the skillet and simmer 15 minutes.

3. Stir in the rice and chicken stock and bring to a boil. Reduce heat, cover, and simmer for 25–30 minutes or until rice is tender. Taste and correct the seasoning. Serve paella hot as an accompaniment to roasted or grilled meats or as a light Sunday supper accompanied by a well-seasoned green salad.

4 tablespoons olive oil

1 small fresh cayenne pepper or 1 small dry red chili pepper, broken

1 large Bermuda onion, peeled, quartered, and thinly sliced

1 large red bell pepper, cored, seeded, and thinly sliced

1 large green bell pepper, cored, seeded, and thinly sliced

2 large cloves garlic, peeled and minced

1½ teaspoons imported paprika

1 tablespoon fresh thyme leaves

1 medium zucchini, trimmed and cubed

4 large ripe tomatoes, peeled, seeded, and chopped

Salt and freshly ground black pepper

1¼ cups rice (preferably Italian-style)

2 cups Chicken Stock (page 37) or bouillon

SERVES 4–6

Warm Mozzarella & Beefsteak Tomato Salad

2 ripe medium Beefsteak tomatoes

8 ounces whole-milk mozzarella, cut crosswise into 12 rectangles about ¼-inch thick

8 teaspoons olive oil, preferably extra-virgin

Coarse salt

Freshly ground black pepper

2 teaspoons fresh thyme leaves

8 thin slices prosciutto or smoked ham

12 fresh basil leaves

SERVES 4

BOUQUET GARNI

To compose Bouquet Garni, tie together 2–3 sprigs Italian parsley, 1 small celery stalk, 1 bay leaf and 1 large sprig thyme.

P·R·E·P·A·R·A·T·I·O·N

1. Cut each tomato crosswise into ¼-inch slices, about 12 slices per tomato; do not include end slices. Set aside.

2. Cut each slice of mozzarella in half crosswise. Reserve.

3. Preheat broiler.

4. On each of 4 individual ovenproof serving plates place 6 slices of tomato and 6 slices of mozzarella, alternating each in an overlapping pattern to form a circle.

5. Drizzle each "circle" with 1 teaspoon olive oil. Sprinkle each with coarse salt, a grinding of black pepper, and ½ teaspoon thyme leaves.

6. Set the plates under the preheated broiler very close to the source of heat. Broil until the mozzarella is just heated through but not melting. Be careful not to burn.

7. Remove plates from broiler. Drizzle each plate with an additional teaspoon of olive oil directly on the outer rim of the plate (the oil will heat through automatically and seep underneath the tomatoes and mozzarella).

8. Drape 2 slices of prosciutto or smoked ham over each and garnish with 3 basil leaves. Serve at once, accompanied by a loaf of French bread and a bowl of sweet butter.

Ziti with Stewed Tomatoes & Steamed Mussels

1. In a large casserole, combine the shallots, white wine, bouquet garni, and mussels. Bring to a boil, reduce heat, cover, and simmer until the mussels have opened. Discard any that do not. Set aside to cool. Remove the mussels to a side dish with a slotted spoon and reserve.

2. Place the casserole with mussel broth over high heat. Bring to a boil and cook until the broth has reduced to ½ cup. Strain through a double layer of cheesecloth and set aside.

3. In a large heavy skillet, heat 2 tablespoons olive oil over medium heat. Add the bacon and cook until lightly browned. Remove with a slotted spoon to a side dish and reserve.

4. Discard all but 2 tablespoons fat from the skillet and add the remaining oil. Add the minced garlic and parsley and cook for 30 seconds.

5. Immediately add the tomatoes, reduced broth, oregano, salt, and pepper. Bring to a boil, reduce heat, partially cover, and simmer for 20–25 minutes. If the sauce seems too thin, whisk in bits of the beurre manié until the sauce lightly coats a spoon. Add the mussels in their shells and the bacon and just heat through. Taste and correct the seasoning. Keep warm.

6. Bring plenty of lightly salted water to a boil in a large pot. Add the ziti and cook for about 10 minutes or until barely tender. As soon as the pasta is done, add 2 cups cold water to the pot to stop further cooking. Drain well. Pour into a deep serving dish and toss with the mussel sauce. Garnish with the minced parsley and serve at once with plenty of napkins and a crusty loaf of French bread.

3 large shallots, peeled and finely minced

½ cup dry white wine

1 Bouquet Garni (page 100)

3 dozen small fresh mussels, well scrubbed

5 tablespoons olive oil, preferably extra-virgin

½ cup lean diced bacon

3 medium cloves garlic, peeled and finely minced

3 tablespoons minced parsley

5–6 large ripe tomatoes peeled, seeded, and chopped

1 tablespoon fresh oregano

Salt and freshly ground black pepper

Optional: *Beurre Manié* (page 54)

½ pound ziti

GARNISH

3 tablespoons finely minced fresh parsley

SERVES 4–6

Fricassee of Chicken with Stewed Tomatoes & Fresh Herbs

9–12 plum tomatoes, peeled

Salt

1 whole 3-pound chicken, cut in eighths

4 tablespoons olive oil, preferably extra-virgin

2 teaspoons butter

Freshly ground black pepper

2 tablespoons finely minced shallots

⅓ cup dry white wine

2 teaspoons tomato paste

½–¾ cup Chicken Stock (page 37) or bouillon

1 Bouquet Garni (page 100)

2 large cloves garlic, peeled and crushed

2 teaspoons fresh oregano

2 teaspoons fresh thyme

1 sprig fresh basil

2 red bell peppers, roasted, peeled (page 65), and thinly sliced

GARNISH

Finely minced fresh parsley

SERVES 4

P·R·E·P·A·R·A·T·I·O·N

1. With the tip of a sharp knife make 2 tiny slits in each tomato. Place in a colander, sprinkle with salt, and let drain one hour.

2. Meanwhile, dry the chicken pieces thoroughly on paper towels. In a 12-inch chicken fryer heat 2 tablespoons oil and the butter over medium-high heat. When the fat is very hot, add the chicken and sauté, partially covered, until nicely browned on all sides. Season with salt and pepper and transfer to a side dish.

3. Discard all but 2 tablespoons of fat from the skillet. Add the shallots and cook for 2 minutes until lightly browned.

4. Add the wine, bring to a boil, and cook until reduced to 1 tablespoon. Add the tomato paste and ½ cup stock. Bring to a boil and reduce heat.

5. Return chicken pieces to the skillet, burying the bouquet garni among them. Cover and simmer for 30 minutes, adding 2–3 tablespoons of stock every 10 minutes.

6. While the chicken is braising, heat the remaining oil in a small skillet. Add the drained tomatoes, garlic, oregano, thyme, and basil sprig. Stew the tomatoes gently over low heat for 10 minutes, or until they have rendered all their juices but are not falling apart.

7. After 30 minutes add the stewed tomatoes and the peppers to the skillet. Simmer covered for another 10 minutes.

8. With a slotted spoon transfer the chicken, tomatoes, and peppers to a serving platter. Discard the bouquet. Increase the heat and cook the pan juices until well reduced and the sauce coats a spoon.

9. Taste the sauce and correct the seasoning, adding a large grinding of black pepper. Spoon it over the chicken and garnish with parsley. Serve at once.

Grilled Tomato Salsa

P·R·E·P·A·R·A·T·I·O·N

1. In a medium mixing bowl, combine the tomatoes, jalapeños, onion, coriander, and garlic. Add the olive oil and lime juice. Mix well. Season with salt and pepper and set aside for 1–2 hours to develop flavor, or store in a covered jar in the refrigerator. The salsa will keep up to 2 weeks; bring back to room temperature before serving.

2. Serve as an accompaniment to grilled meats, omelettes such as the Corn & Cheddar Cheese Omelettes (page 42), or with fried tortilla triangles.

R·E·M·A·R·K·S

I often add 1 cup of the tomato salsa to 2 cups of well-flavored mayonnaise and serve it as an accompaniment to grilled fish or shellfish.

To roast tomatoes: Place whole, unpeeled tomatoes over hot coals of a charcoal grill, high flame of a gas stove, or directly on hot coils of an electric stove. Roast until the skin is charred on all sides. Remove and, when cool enough to handle, peel off charred skin, cut in half, and remove seeds.

4 ripe medium tomatoes (about 1½ pounds), roasted, peeled (see remarks), and diced

2 jalapeño peppers, roasted, peeled (page 65), and finely diced

3 tablespoons finely minced red onion

2 tablespoons finely minced fresh coriander (cilantro)

1 large clove garlic, peeled and mashed

3 tablespoons olive oil, preferably extra-virgin

Juice of 1 small lime

Salt and freshly ground black pepper

MAKES ABOUT 1½ CUPS

BURPEE'S

ZUCCHINI
SUMMER SQUASH

The prolific ways of the zucchini plant are nearly legendary. If gardeners have any problem with this irrepressible vegetable, it is finding enough takers for the inevitable surplus.

Personally, I never tire of zucchini and the other types of summer squash. With their delicate and unassertive flavors, they are among the most versatile of vegetables. Sautéed, fried, steamed, pureed, stuffed, served cold in salads or even raw, they lend themselves to endless preparations one of which is my all-time favorite vegetable dish: a plateful of zucchini slivers fried to crisp perfection. Yellow crookneck and straightneck types, and the scalloped, round patty pans, offer delightful variations of shapes and colors for the summer kitchen.

Summer squash is so productive, it is best to limit yourself to just a few plants each of your two or three favorite types. Much like cucumbers, summer squash do not allow even a single day of laziness in picking; one day the fruit is just short of perfect size, and the next thing you know, a giant squash lies heavily on the ground. Some gardeners feel a certain pride at being able to grow giant specimens of summer squash, not realizing that as the fruit gains in size so will it begin to lose its flavor. Now, with the new emphasis on smaller and younger vegetables, many gardening cooks are discovering that great tastes come in small packages.

My favorite time to pick summer squash is at the "baby" stage. Harvested at this prime moment, zucchini and yellow squash offer crisp, distinctive flavors rather than the watery, bland tastes associated with the mature fruit. For sautéing, braising, or for use in salads, I pick the zucchini at no more than four inches in length, at which point they are still wonderfully sweet.

Baby squashes can be picked so young that their yellow flowers are still attached. But be careful; bees love to nestle inside the blooms. Italians have a wonderful way of stuffing the flowers with diced mozzarella, minced herbs, and some anchovies or prosciutto. Entire zucchini, flowers included, are dipped in a light batter and then deep-fried. This makes for one of the most tantalizing appetizers of the summer season.

Due to their high water content, summer squashes should be salted and allowed to drain for certain preparations. I always salt grated zucchini, letting it dry over a colander for an hour or two. Sliced zucchini need salting only if they are large or are to be incorporated into a custard or egg batter, where excess moisture may change the texture of the dish. For salads and stuffed squash, it is best to blanch the zucchini first to remove some of the raw crunchiness while retaining the crispness without overcooking. Both yellow and green squashes make delectable pickles.

S · T · O · R · A · G · E

Refrigerate summer squash in plastic bags. The fruit will keep well for three to five days.

G · A · R · D · E · N · I · N · G

Unlike many winter squashes, which grow along sprawling ten-foot-long vines, most summer squashes grow on bushlike plants suitable even for small-sized gardens. Like the closely related cucumber, squash plants are extremely sensitive to cold and should not be set out until the soil warms up and all danger of frost has passed. Squash have finicky root systems and do not transplant very well. Therefore, sow seeds directly in the garden rather than indoors first. If you must use transplants, protect them with Hot-kaps immediately after planting.

Some people say it is easier to keep squash seedlings properly moist when grown in "hills," or mounds, but I have had good luck planting them in rows. Either way it is imperative to condition the soil with a generous amount of well-rotted manure or compost.

Summer squashes are among the crops ideally suited for growing on plastic mulch. The plastic keeps soil moisture in and weeds out and protects the fruit against insects and rotting. I usually apply mulch in between the squash rows soon after thinning my seedlings. Even with mulch, the plants are subject to destructive borers as well as to mildew and "wilt" diseases. Where space permits, sow a second crop by midsummer to help guarantee harvests until frost. Do not plant squash in the same spots where previous plantings have been affected by wilt.

For excellent flavor it is difficult to surpass Burpee Hybrid Zucchini. The bushlike plants yield an abundance of medium-green fruit starting just fifty days after planting. Pic-N-Pic Hybrid, a golden yellow crookneck squash, also takes fifty days and, as the name suggests, it is extremely prolific. Be sure to pick crook-necks while they are young and small, before the "handles" get hard. Another fine addition to the garden is Butterstick Hybrid, a new yellow straightneck type. It has a somewhat nuttier taste than zucchini and a firmer, drier texture.

H · A · R · V · E · S · T · I · N · G

Always use pruning shears or a sharp knife rather than twisting squash fruit off by hand. Continuous picking promotes non-stop production.

SWEET AND SOUR PICKLED SUMMER SQUASH

In a large bowl, combine 4 quarts cold water and 1 cup pickling lime. Add 4 pounds yellow squash, cut into ⅛-inch slices. Soak overnight in refrigerator. Drain; rinse well. Place in a large bowl and cover with ice water. Soak three hours. Combine 5 cups granulated sugar, 4 cups cider vinegar, 1 tablespoon salt, ½ teaspoon whole cloves, ½ teaspoon whole allspice, and ½ teaspoon celery seed in large pot. Bring to a boil. Drain squash, pour hot vinegar/sugar mixture over and let sit 6 hours. Simmer squash in mixture for 25 minutes. Pack slices in sterilized jars and fill with hot syrup, leaving ½-inch headspace. Cover and process 5 minutes in boiling water bath. Store in cool place. Makes 6–8 pints.

R·E·C·I·P·E·S

Stir-Fried Zucchini with Garlic & Basil 109

Sweet-and-Sour Braised Summer Squash 110

Zucchini "Pasta" Alfredo 111

Zucchini & Plum Tomato Salad in Basil Vinaigrette 112

Pilaf of Zucchini with Tomato Fondue 113

"Grilled" Summer Squash & Tomato Casserole 114

Greek Yellow Zucchini & Lemon Soup 115

Sauté of Chicken with Tomatoes, Zucchini & Pesto 116

Crisp Zucchini Pancakes 117

Stuffed Zucchini with Tuna & Rice à l'Italienne 118

Fusilli with Sautéed Shrimp, Ginger & Zucchini Sauce 119

Baked Zucchini with Grilled Peppers & Mozzarella 120

Cream of Zucchini, Tomato & Basil Soup 121

Stir-Fried Zucchini with Garlic & Basil

P·R·E·P·A·R·A·T·I·O·N

1. Cut the zucchini in half lengthwise and with a grapefruit spoon scoop out the seedy center, as if seeding a cucumber. Cut the seeded zucchini crosswise into ¼-inch slices.

2. In a large heavy skillet heat the olive oil over medium-high heat. Add the zucchini, season with salt and pepper, and sauté quickly, tossing the zucchini constantly in the oil for 2 minutes. Add the garlic and basil and cook for 30 seconds longer; the zucchini should still be crisp. Taste and correct the seasoning and serve at once.

4 medium zucchini, trimmed

3 tablespoons olive oil

Salt and freshly ground black
 pepper

2 large cloves garlic, peeled and
 finely minced

6 large fresh basil leaves, cut into a
 fine julienne

SERVES 4–5

R·E·M·A·R·K·S

For a lovely contrast of color, use both green and yellow zucchini or straight-neck squash in this recipe.

Sweet-and-Sour Braised Summer Squash

2 tablespoons red wine vinegar

2 teaspoons granulated sugar

9 tablespoons olive oil

4–5 medium zucchini (about 1½ pounds), trimmed, cut in half lengthwise, then cut lengthwise into ¼-inch strips

Flour for dredging

3 medium cloves garlic, peeled and finely minced

Salt and freshly ground black pepper

Optional: 2 tablespoons pine nuts

GARNISH

2–3 tablespoons finely minced fresh parsley

SERVES 4

P·R·E·P·A·R·A·T·I·O·N

1. Combine the vinegar and sugar in a small bowl and set aside.

2. Dry the zucchini thoroughly on paper towels. Dredge lightly in flour, shaking off the excess.

3. Heat 3 tablespoons oil in a large skillet over medium-high heat. Add half the zucchini and sauté until nicely browned. Remove with a slotted spoon to a side dish. Add 3 more tablespoons oil to the skillet and sauté remaining zucchini. Remove and set aside.

4. Wipe skillet clean. Heat remaining oil, add the garlic, and cook for 1 minute without browning. Add the vinegar/sugar mixture and sautéed zucchini. Season with salt and pepper, cover, and just heat through. Set aside.

5. If using pine nuts, sauté quickly in a small skillet with 1 tablespoon oil until lightly browned. Add to zucchini, sprinkle with minced parsley, and serve at once directly from the skillet.

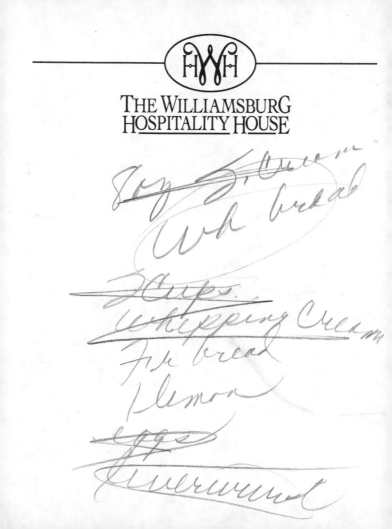

Sour cream
~~Wh bread~~

~~Cups~~
~~whipping cream~~
Fr bread
lemon
~~eggs~~
~~_____~~

Zucchini "Pasta" Alfredo

1. In a medium saucepan, bring the cream to a boil. Reduce heat and continue to simmer until reduced by half. Season with salt and pepper and set aside.

2. Cut the zucchini lengthwise into ⅛-inch slices. Stack the slices and cut lengthwise into ⅛-inch strips, avoiding as much of the seedy or center part of the zucchini as possible.

3. Sauté the zucchini in 2 batches. In a large heavy skillet melt 2 tablespoons butter over medium heat. Add ½ the shallots and ½ the zucchini strips and cook for 1 minute or until barely tender. The zucchini should still be slightly crisp. Remove from the pan with a slotted spoon. Add the remaining shallots and 2 tablespoons more butter and when hot add the remaining zucchini and again cook till slightly crisp.

4. Combine the 2 batches of zucchini in the skillet. Add the reduced cream, Parmesan, and remaining butter and cook for 1 minute longer. Taste and correct the seasoning, adding a large grinding of black pepper. Serve as a vegetable with roast or grilled meats, garnished with a sprinkling of finely minced Italian parsley and grated Parmesan.

1 cup heavy cream
Salt and freshly ground black pepper
2 medium green zucchini and 2 medium yellow zucchini, trimmed and cut in half crosswise
6 tablespoons unsalted butter
2 medium shallots, peeled and finely minced
3–4 tablespoons coarsely grated Parmesan cheese

GARNISH

Finely minced Italian parsley
Bowl of freshly grated Parmesan cheese

SERVES 6

V·A·R·I·A·T·I·O·N·S

1. Add ½ pound large mushrooms, stems removed and caps cut into a ¼-inch julienne. Sauté separately in 2 tablespoons butter and add to the finished dish.

2. You may also add to the sauce 12 large basil leaves cut into a fine julienne and 2 tablespoons finely minced fresh chives.

3. For another variation, add 1 large red pepper, roasted, peeled, and cut into a fine julienne to match that of the zucchini.

Zucchini & Plum Tomato Salad in Basil Vinaigrette

THE DRESSING

⅓ cup olive oil, preferably extra-virgin

2 tablespoons red wine vinegar

1 large clove garlic, peeled and mashed

4 tablespoons finely minced fresh basil

THE ZUCCHINI AND TOMATOES

6 small zucchini, trimmed

Juice of 1 large lemon

Salt and freshly ground black pepper

1 small red onion, peeled and thinly sliced

3 tablespoons finely minced fresh parsley

½ cup finely diced red bell pepper or pimientos

6 ripe Italian plum tomatoes, quartered

SERVES 6

P·R·E·P·A·R·A·T·I·O·N

1. Start by making *the dressing:* In a small jar combine the olive oil, vinegar, garlic, and basil. Shake the jar to blend well and chill for 30 minutes.

2. Bring 4 quarts of salted water to a boil in a large saucepan, add the zucchini, and cook over medium heat for 5–7 minutes, or until they are easily pierced with the tip of a sharp knife, taking care not to overcook. As soon as the zucchini are done, run under cold water to stop further cooking. Drain and place on a double layer of paper towels to cool.

3. When cool enough to handle, cut the zucchini in half lengthwise and then in half crosswise and sprinkle with lemon juice, salt, and pepper. Set aside.

4. An hour or two before serving, sprinkle the zucchini with the onion rings, parsley, and red pepper or pimiento. Arrange the quartered tomatoes around them and pour the dressing over both vegetables. Season with salt and freshly ground black pepper. Serve chilled.

Pilaf of Zucchini with Tomato Fondue

1. Place the zucchini in a colander, sprinkle with salt, and let drain for 30 minutes. Dry thoroughly with paper towels.

2. In a large heavy skillet heat 3 tablespoons olive oil over medium-high heat. Add the zucchini and cook, stirring often, until nicely browned on all sides. Remove with a slotted spoon to a side dish and reserve.

3. In a heavy skillet or 3-quart casserole heat the butter and remaining oil over medium heat. Add the shallots and cook for 1–2 minutes, until soft but not browned. Add the tomatoes and season with salt and pepper. Cook, stirring often, until all the tomato juices have evaporated.

4. Add the rice and toss to coat evenly with the tomato mixture. Add the stock to the casserole, cover, and cook for 25–30 minutes or until rice is tender.

5. When done, taste and correct the seasoning. Add the reserved zucchini, Parmesan cheese, parsley, and optional butter and fold gently into the rice. Serve as a first course or as an accompaniment to roast or grilled meats with a side dish of Parmesan cheese and a crusty loaf of bread.

3 small zucchini, trimmed and cut
  into ½-inch cubes

Salt

4 tablespoons olive oil

3 tablespoons unsalted butter

¼ cup finely minced shallots

6–8 Italian plum tomatoes, peeled
  and cut crosswise into ¼-inch
  slices

Freshly ground black pepper

1 cup rice, preferably Italian-style

2–2½ cups homemade Chicken
  Stock (page 37) or bouillon

⅓–½ cup freshly grated Parmesan
  cheese

¼ cup finely minced fresh parsley

Optional: 2 tablespoons unsalted
  butter

SERVES 4–6

"Grilled" Summer Squash & Tomato Casserole

4 tablespoons olive oil

3 medium zucchini (about 1½ pounds), trimmed and cut on the diagonal into ⅓-inch slices

6 small ripe tomatoes (about 1½ pounds), cored and cut crosswise into ⅓-inch slices

2 large cloves garlic, peeled and thinly sliced

12 tiny fresh basil leaves

Coarse salt

Freshly ground black pepper

SERVES 6

1. Prepare the charcoal grill, concentrating the coals on one side only.

2. Brush the bottom and sides of a 2-quart gratin dish or oval baking dish with 1 tablespoon olive oil.

3. Arrange the zucchini and tomato slices in the baking dish in alternating and tightly overlapping rows. Tuck the slices of garlic and basil leaves between the rows. Sprinkle with coarse salt, pepper, and drizzle with the remaining olive oil.

4. Cover tightly with aluminum foil. Place the dish on the grill but not directly over the coals and cook for 10 minutes. Uncover and cook for another 10–15 minutes or until the juices have evaporated and vegetables are tender. Remove from the grill and serve warm or at room temperature.

R·E·M·A·R·K·S

Since the casserole does not cook directly over the coals, you can grill meat or fish simultaneously with the casserole to accompany it. The casserole can be baked rather than grilled. Place in a 350°F oven and bake for 35–40 minutes.

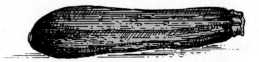

Greek Yellow Zucchini & Lemon Soup

P·R·E·P·A·R·A·T·I·O·N

1. In a large casserole melt the butter over medium heat. Add the onion and cook until soft but not browned. Add the zucchini, season with salt and pepper, reduce heat, cover, and simmer for 10 minutes.

2. Add 5 cups chicken stock, bring to a boil, reduce heat, cover, and simmer for 15 minutes longer or until zucchini is very soft.

3. Cool the soup and puree until quite smooth in a food processor or blender. Return to the casserole. Bring back to a boil, add the orzo, reduce heat, and cook until the orzo is quite tender, about 7–8 minutes.

4. In a small bowl combine the heavy cream, egg yolks, and lemon juice and whisk until smooth.

5. Reduce heat under soup to low, add the cream/egg yolk mixture, and whisk until well blended. Do not let come to a boil or egg yolks will curdle. Add the mint and julienne of zucchini and cook until just heated through. Taste and correct the seasoning. If soup is too thick, add the remaining stock. Serve at once.

R·E·M·A·R·K·S

The soup may be made in advance to the point of adding the cream/yolk serving. This should be added just before serving. Bring soup back to a boil, reduce heat to low, and proceed.

4 tablespoons unsalted butter

1 large onion, peeled and finely minced

3–4 medium yellow zucchini or other summer squash (about 1½ pounds), trimmed, cut in half lengthwise, then cut crosswise into ½-inch slices

Salt and freshly ground white pepper

5–6 cups Chicken Stock (page 37) or bouillon

¼ cup orzo, riso, or other rice-shaped pasta

½ cup heavy cream

2 egg yolks

Juice of 1 large lemon

2 tablespoons finely minced fresh mint

GARNISH

1 medium yellow zucchini or other summer squash, skin only, cut into a fine julienne

SERVES 6

Sauté of Chicken with Tomatoes, Zucchini & Pesto

1 whole 3–3½-pound chicken cut
  into eighths
Salt and freshly ground black
  pepper
Flour for dredging
5 tablespoons olive oil, preferably
  extra-virgin
2 large shallots, peeled and finely
  minced
½ cup dry white wine
3 large ripe tomatoes, peeled,
  seeded, and chopped
1 teaspoon tomato paste
1 Bouquet Garni (page 100)
1 cup Chicken Stock (page 37) or
  bouillon
3 medium zucchini, trimmed
2 large cloves garlic, peeled and
  finely minced
1 Beurre Manié (page 54)
2 tablespoons Basil Paste (page 20)

GARNISH

2 tablespoons minced fresh parsley

SERVES 4–5

P·R·E·P·A·R·A·T·I·O·N

1. Dry the chicken thoroughly on paper towels. Season with salt and pepper and dredge lightly in flour, shaking off the excess.

2. In a 12-inch chicken fryer, heat 2 tablespoons olive oil over medium-high heat. When the oil is very hot, add the chicken and sauté, partially covered, until the pieces are nicely browned on all sides. Transfer to a side dish.

3. Discard all the fat from the skillet and add 2 more tablespoons olive oil. Add the shallots and cook until soft and lightly browned. Add the white wine and cook until reduced to 2 tablespoons. Add the tomatoes, tomato paste, bouquet garni, and ½ cup chicken stock. Season with salt and pepper.

4. Return the dark pieces of chicken (thighs, drumsticks) to the skillet, reduce heat, cover, and simmer for 15 minutes. Add the white pieces of chicken (breasts) to the skillet and continue cooking for 15 minutes longer or until all the pieces are done (the juices will run pale yellow).

5. While the chicken is braising, *prepare the zucchini:* Cut the zucchini in half lengthwise and with a grapefruit spoon scoop out the seedy center, as if seeding a cucumber. Cut the seeded zucchini crosswise into ¼-inch slices.

6. In a heavy 10-inch skillet, heat the remaining olive oil over medium-high heat. Add the zucchini, season with salt and pepper, and sauté quickly, tossing the zucchini constantly in the oil for 2 minutes. Add the garlic and cook for 30 seconds longer. Remove with a slotted spoon and set aside.

7. When the chicken is done, transfer it to a serving platter and keep warm. Remove and discard the bouquet. Add the remaining stock to the skillet, bring to a boil, and reduce by ⅓. Whisk in bits of beurre manié until the sauce lightly coats a spoon. Add the sautéed zucchini/garlic mixture and basil paste and just heat through. Taste and correct the seasoning.

8. Spoon the sauce over the chicken, sprinkle with minced parsley, and serve at once.

Crisp Zucchini Pancakes

P·R·E·P·A·R·A·T·I·O·N

1. Place the zucchini in a colander. Sprinkle lightly with salt and let drain for 30 minutes. With a wooden spoon press as much liquid as you can from the zucchini. Set aside.

2. In a small skillet, melt the butter. Add the onion and sauté over medium heat until soft but not browned.

3. Combine the zucchini, onion, eggs, and flour in a large mixing bowl and mix until well blended. Season to taste with salt and pepper.

4. Heat oil to a depth of ¼ inch in a heavy skillet over medium to medium-high heat. When hot, add the zucchini mixture by heaping tablespoonfuls to the oil without crowding the skillet. Flatten out each a bit with the back of a spoon. Cook for about 1 minute on each side or until nicely browned.

5. Transfer the pancakes with a slotted spoon to a double layer of paper towels to drain. Sprinkle with salt and pepper. Serve at once.

3 medium zucchini (about 1 pound), trimmed and shredded
Salt
2 tablespoons unsalted butter
1 medium onion, peeled and finely minced
2 large eggs, lightly beaten
¼ cup all-purpose flour
Freshly ground black pepper
Vegetable oil for frying

MAKES 14–16 PANCAKES

Stuffed Zucchini with Tuna & Rice à l'Italienne

3 large zucchini, trimmed

3 tablespoons unsalted butter

½ cup finely minced onion

½ cup rice, preferably Italian-style

1½ cups Chicken Stock (page 37) or bouillon

Salt and freshly ground black pepper

3 tablespoons finely minced fresh parsley

3 tablespoons finely minced roasted bell peppers (page 65) or pimientos

3 tablespoons Basil Paste (page 20)

Optional: 4 anchovy fillets, finely minced

3 ounces light tuna, drained and flaked

3–5 tablespoons olive oil, preferably extra-virgin

GARNISH

Tiny fresh basil leaves

SERVES 6

P·R·E·P·A·R·A·T·I·O·N

1. Cut the zucchini crosswise into 1½-inch pieces. Place the pieces on a cutting surface, cut sides down. With a tip of a small knife, scoop out the center of each, leaving the walls and bottom of each zucchini ¼-inch thick.

2. Bring water to a boil in a vegetable steamer, add the zucchini, cover, and steam for 3 minutes. Remove and reserve.

3. In a 1-quart saucepan, melt the butter over medium heat. Add the onion and cook until soft but not browned. Add the rice and 1 cup stock. Season with salt and pepper, bring to a boil, reduce heat, and simmer covered for 20 minutes or until rice is tender and all the broth has been absorbed.

4. Transfer the rice to a large mixing bowl. Add the parsley, roasted pepper or pimiento, basil paste, optional anchovies, and tuna. Fold the mixture thoroughly into the rice. Taste and correct the seasoning.

5. Fill each zucchini cavity with some of the filling. Place filled side up in a baking dish, drizzle with olive oil, and add remaining chicken broth. Cover tightly.

6. Preheat oven to 350°F.

7. Place baking dish in the center of the preheated oven and bake for 30 minutes or until zucchini are just tender. You may need to add a little more stock to the baking dish if the juices run dry.

8. Serve the zucchini warm or at room temperature sprinkled with a little fruity olive oil and freshly ground black pepper. Garnish with fresh basil leaves.

Fusilli with Sautéed Shrimp, Ginger & Zucchini Sauce

1. In a large heavy skillet heat 2 tablespoons olive oil over medium-high heat. When the oil is hot, add the cayenne pepper and shrimp without crowding the pan and sauté until bright pink and lightly browned. Immediately remove from the skillet with a slotted spoon, discard cayenne pepper, and set aside.

2. Reduce the heat, add 2 tablespoons oil to the skillet, and add the garlic, ginger, and shallots. Cook until shallots are soft but not browned.

3. Add the tomatoes, oregano, thyme, salt, and pepper. Reduce heat, cover, and simmer until the ginger is very soft.

4. In another heavy skillet, heat the remaining oil over medium-high heat. Add the zucchini and sauté quickly until lightly browned. Season with salt and pepper and add to the tomato sauce. Simmer for 5 minutes. Keep the sauce warm.

5. Dice the shrimp and set aside.

6. Bring plenty of lightly salted water to a boil in a large pot. Add the fusilli and cook until just tender (al dente). Immediately add 2 cups cold water to the pot to stop further cooking.

7. Add the diced shrimp to the tomato/zucchini sauce and remove from the heat.

8. Drain the pasta well, return to the pot, and toss with the shrimp, zucchini, and ginger sauce. Add the basil and minced parsley. Taste and correct the seasoning, adding a large grinding of black pepper. Serve at once with a loaf of crusty French bread.

6 tablespoons olive oil

1 small fresh cayenne pepper or 1 dried chili pepper

½ pound small shrimp, peeled

2 large cloves garlic, peeled and finely minced

1½ teaspoons finely minced fresh gingerroot

6 small shallots, peeled and thinly sliced

4 large ripe tomatoes, peeled, seeded, and chopped

2 teaspoons fresh oregano

2 teaspoons fresh thyme

Salt and freshly ground black pepper

2 small zucchini, quartered lengthwise and thinly sliced

½ pound fusilli, rotelle, or twists

4 tablespoons finely minced fresh basil

2 tablespoons finely minced Italian parsley

SERVES 4–5

Baked Zucchini with Grilled Peppers & Mozzarella

3 medium zucchini, trimmed and
  cut in half crosswise

All-purpose flour for dredging

4–6 tablespoons olive oil

Salt and freshly ground black
  pepper

½ pound mozzarella, partially
  frozen and cut into ¼-inch slices

1 cup Tomato and Shallot Fondue
  (page 93)

1 large green bell pepper, roasted,
  peeled (page 65), and thinly
  sliced into 1½-inch-long strips

Optional: 6–8 anchovy fillets, cut
  in half lengthwise and then in
  half crosswise

2 teaspoons fresh thyme

2 teaspoons fresh oregano

GARNISH

Sprigs of Italian parsley

SERVES 6–8

*The baked zucchini is equally
delicious served at room temperature
as part of an hors d'oeuvre table,
garnished with black oil-cured olives,
pitted and cut in half.*

P·R·E·P·A·R·A·T·I·O·N

1. Preheat oven to 375°F.

2. Cut the zucchini lengthwise into ¼-inch slices. Dredge lightly in flour, shaking off the excess. Set aside.

3. In a large heavy skillet heat 2 tablespoons olive oil over medium-high heat. When hot, add the zucchini slices without crowding the pan (this will have to be done in several batches). Cook until nicely browned, then turn slices over and cook until nicely browned on the other side. Transfer to a double layer of paper towels to drain. Continue frying the remaining zucchini slices, adding a little more oil each time to the skillet. Season with salt and pepper.

4. Cut the mozzarella slices into pieces—the same size as the zucchini slices—and reserve.

5. Place the zucchini into a single layer in a shallow baking dish. Top each slice with a little tomato fondue and sprinkle with the grilled pepper. Place a slice of mozzarella on each and garnish with a piece of the optional anchovy. Sprinkle with thyme, oregano, and a good grinding of black pepper.

6. Place the baking dish in the center of the preheated oven and bake for 15 minutes or until cheese has melted and is bubbly.

7. Remove from the oven and let cool for 5 minutes. Garnish with sprigs of Italian parsley and serve as a vegetable accompaniment.

Cream of Zucchini, Tomato & Basil Soup

P·R·E·P·A·R·A·T·I·O·N

1. In a 3-quart casserole heat the butter. Add the onion, garlic, and zucchini and simmer the mixture over low heat for 2–3 minutes without browning.

2. Add the tomatoes, oregano, and stock. Season with salt and a large grinding of black pepper. Bring to a boil, reduce heat, and simmer the soup for 35 minutes or until the vegetables are very tender.

3. Cool the soup and puree in a food processor or blender until smooth. Return the soup to the saucepan and add the julienne of zucchini. Simmer just until zucchini is crisp tender.

4. Add the sour cream or crème fraîche, heat through, and correct seasoning. Just before serving, add the basil paste.

5. Serve the soup hot, accompanied by French bread, or slightly chilled, garnished with diced tomato and tiny basil leaves.

R·E·M·A·R·K·S

This soup can be made well in advance and reheated. It also freezes well. To retain the true flavor of summer freshness, it is always best to add the basil at the last minute.

4 tablespoons unsalted butter

1 large onion, peeled and finely minced

1 large clove garlic, peeled and mashed

3 medium zucchini, cut in half and finely sliced

2 pounds ripe tomatoes, peeled, seeded, and coarsely chopped

2 tablespoons fresh oregano

4 cups Chicken Stock (page 37) or bouillon

Salt and freshly ground black pepper

1 cup zucchini, skins only, cut into julienne

½ cup sour cream or Crème Fraîche (page 57)

2 tablespoons Basil Paste (page 20)

GARNISH

Finely diced fresh tomato

Tiny basil leaves

SERVES 6

basil:
  dressing, green bean and pasta salad with, 21
  paste, 20
  a soup of mixed beans alla Milanese with pastina and, 20
  stir-fried zucchini with garlic and, 109
  vinaigrette, zucchini and plum tomato salad in, 112
  zucchini and tomato soup, cream of, 121
beef and pepper soup, hearty Viennese, 70
beurre manié, 54
bouquet garni, 100

carrot(s), 22–25
  braised cucumbers and, with tarragon cream, 57
  and cabbage slaw, creamy, 31
  clafoutis, 28
  glazed, with brown sugar and mint, 26
  grated, and pineapple muffins, 33
  puree of, with crème fraîche and honey, 29
  rice pilaf of golden raisins and, 32
  roast pork with prunes and, in sweet port wine sauce, 30–31
  soup with fragrant Indian spices, 27
cheese:
  cheddar, and corn omelettes, 42
  cream, cherry tomatoes with curry filling, 94
  goat, cucumber boats with summer herbs and, 59
  mozzarella, baked zucchini with grilled peppers and, 120
  mozzarella, warm, and beefsteak tomato salad, 100
chicken:
  breasts, sauté of, in lemon and cucumber sauce, 58
  fricassee of, with stewed tomatoes and fresh herbs, 102–3
  sauté of, with tomatoes, zucchini and pesto, 116–17
  stock, 37

wings, southern fried, with spicy corn relish, 47
corn, 34–37
  and cheddar cheese omelettes, 42
  chowder, summer's best, 39
  and egg "flower" soup, 38
  relish, 47
  and roasted pepper dressing, 45
  salad Mexicane, 44–45
  sauté of, and shrimp Indienne, 46
  sour cream bread, 41
  -studded polenta, 43
  and zucchini fritters, 40
crème fraîche, 57
  purree of carrots with honey and, 29
cucumber(s), 48–52
  boats with goat cheese and summer herbs, 59
  braised carrots and, with tarragon cream, 57
  and lemon sauce, sauté of chicken breasts in, 58
  overnight crunchy pickles, 53
  salad, ever-so-sweet Viennese, 54
  salad, minted Middle Eastern, 55
  shrimp and mushroom salad in mustard and dill mayonnaise, 61
  and sour cream dip, zesty mixed, 56
  and tomato sauce, fillets of sole in, 60

egg "flower" and corn soup, 38

fondue:
  garlic and tomato, roast leg of lamb in, 96–97
  tomato, pilaf of zucchini with, 113
  tomato and shallot, 93

gazpacho, Basque, 98

lamb, roast leg of, in garlic and tomato fondue, 96–97

mayonnaise, homemade, 13
minestrone, summer, 97
mint, minted:
  glazed carrots with brown sugar and, 26
  Middle Eastern cucumber salad, 55
muffins, grated carrot and pineapple, 33
mushroom, cucumber and shrimp salad in mustard and dill mayonnaise, 61

mussels, steamed, ziti with stewed tomatoes and, 101

onion(s):
  pepper and anchovy pizza, 67
  sauté of two beans with tomatoes, tuna and, 17

paella, vegetable:
  baked Swiss chard leaves with, 85
Basque, 99
pasta:
  fettuccine with seafood in pepper sauce, 68–69
  fusilli with sautéed shrimp, ginger and zucchini sauce, 119
  and green bean salad with basil dressing, 21
  rigatoni and peppers, tiny boulettes with, 74–75
  ziti with stewed tomatoes and steamed mussels, 101
pepper(s), 62–66
  and beef soup, hearty Viennese, 70
  grilled, baked zucchini with mozzarella and, 120
  Mediterranean stuffed, 72
  onion and anchovy pizza, 67
  pickled hot, Mary's, 73
  and rigatoni, tiny boulettes with, 74–75
  roasted, and corn dressing, 45
  roasted red or green, 65
  salad, Balkan grilled, 71
  sauce, fettuccine with seafood in, 68–69
  spicy sauté of sausages and, 76
  and tomato soup, Basque, 69
  zucchini and potato frittata, 77
pickles, overnight crunchy, 53
pizza, pepper, onion and anchovy, 67
polenta, corn-studded, 43
pork, roast, with carrots and prunes in sweet port wine sauce, 30–31
potato, pepper and zucchini frittata, 77

radish and green bean salad in sour cream vinaigrette, 13
rice:
  baked Swiss chard leaves with vegetable paella, 85
  Basque vegetable paella, 99
  pilaf of carrots and golden raisins, 32
  tomato and dill soup, 95

and tuna à l'Italienne, stuffed zucchini with, 118
of zucchini with tomato fondue, 113

salad:
  bean, Niçoise, 14
  corn, Mexicane, 44–45
  cucumber, ever-so-sweet Viennese, 54
  cucumber, minted Middle Eastern, 55
  cucumber, shrimp and mushroom, in mustard and dill mayonnaise, 61
  green and wax bean, with a mayonnaise vinaigrette, 16
  green bean, warm, with crisp potato circles, 15
  green bean and pasta, with basil dressing, 21
  green bean and radish, in sour cream vinaigrette, 13
  grilled pepper, Balkan, 71
  mozzarella and beefsteak tomato, warm, 100
  zucchini and plum tomato, in basil vinaigrette, 112
sauce:
  classic plum tomato, 92
  grilled tomato salsa, 103
  roasted pepper and corn dressing, 45
sausages, spicy sauté of peppers and, 76
sauté:
  of chicken breast in lemon and cucumber sauce, 58
  of chicken with tomatoes, zucchini and pesto, 116–17
  of peppers and sausages, spicy, 76
  of shrimp and corn Indienne, 46
  of Swiss chard with ginger and garlic, 83
  of two beans with tomatoes, onions and tuna, 17
seafood with fettuccine in pepper sauce, 68–69
shallot and tomato fondue, 93
shrimp:
  cucumber and mushroom salad in mustard and dill mayonnaise, 61
  ginger and zucchini sauce, fusilli with, 119
  sauté of, and corn Indienne, 46
snap beans, 8–12
  bean salad Niçoise, 14

green and wax bean salad with a mayonnaise vinaigrette, 16
green bean and pasta salad with basil dressing, 21
green bean and radish salad in sour cream vinaigrette, 13
pickled green and yellow beans, 11
puree of green beans with sour cream and Parmesan, 19
sauté of two beans with tomatoes, onions and tuna, 17
a soup of mixed beans alla Milanese (with basil and pastina), 20
Viennese green beans in piquant tomato sauce, 18
warm green bean salad with crisp potato circles, 15
sole, fillets of, in cucumber and tomato sauce, 60
soup:
  carrot, with fragrant Indian spices, 27
  egg "flower" and corn, 38
  of mixed beans alla Milanese (with basil and pastina), 20
  pepper and beef, hearty Viennese, 70
  Swiss chard and leek, creamy, 82
  tomato, dill and rice, 95
  tomato and pepper, Basque, 69
  yellow zucchini and lemon, Greek, 115
  zucchini, tomato and basil, cream of, 121
summer squash, 104–7
  sweet-and-sour braised, 110
  sweet-and-sour pickled, 107
  and tomato casserole, "grilled," 114
  see also zucchini
Swiss chard, 78–81
  leaves, baked, with vegetable paella, 85
  and leek soup, creamy, 82
  sauté of, with ginger and garlic, 83
  tart Provençale, sweet, 84

tomato(es), 86–91
  beefsteak, and mozzarella salad, warm, 100
  broiled, Pennsylvania Dutch, 94
  canning, 88
  cherry, with curry cream cheese filling, 94
  and cucumber sauce, fillets of sole in, 60
  dill and rice soup, 95

fondue, pilaf of zucchini with, 113
and garlic fondue, roast leg of lamb in, 96–97
gazpacho, Basque, 98
and pepper soup, Basque, 69
plum, and zucchini salad in basil vinaigrette, 112
salsa, grilled, 103
sauce, classic plum, 92
sauce, piquant, Viennese green beans in, 18
sauté of two beans with onions, tuna and, 17
and shallot fondue, 93
stewed, fricassee of chicken with fresh herbs and, 102–3
stewed, ziti with steamed mussels and, 101
summer minestrone, 97
and summer squash casserole, "grilled," 114
vegetable paella, Basque, 99
zucchini and basil soup, cream of, 121
tuna:
  and rice à l'Italienne, stuffed zucchini with, 118
  sauté of two beans with tomatoes, onions and, 17

vinaigrette, Provençale, 14

zucchini, 104–7
  baked, with grilled peppers and mozzarella, 120
  and corn fritters, 40
  pancakes, crisp, 117
  "pasta" Alfredo, 113
  pepper and potato frittata, 77
  pilaf of, with tomato fondue, 113
  and plum tomato salad in basil vinaigrette, 112
  sauté of chicken with tomatoes, pesto and, 116–17
  shrimp and ginger sauce, fusilli with, 119
  stir-fried, with garlic and basil, 109
  stuffed, with tuna and rice à l'Italienne, 118
  tomato and basil soup, cream of, 121
  yellow, and lemon soup, Greek, 115
  see also summer squash

EARLY SUMMER VEGETABLES	WHEN TO PLANT OR SOW FOR SUMMER CROP	HOW TO PLANT (SPACING)
BEANS		
BUSH SNAP BEANS	After all danger of spring frost, then sow again 2 weeks later	Seeds 2" deep; thin to 4"–6" apart in rows 18"–30" apart
POLE SNAP BEANS	After all danger of spring frost	Seeds 2" deep; thin to 3 or 4 plants around each pole
CARROTS	Spring to early summer; sow every 3–4 weeks for continuous harvest	Seeds ½" deep; thin to 2"–3" apart in rows 1'–2' apart
CORN	After all danger of frost, after air and soil have warmed	Seeds 1" deep; thin to 12" apart in rows 2'–3' apart. Plant at least 4 rows side by side for best ears
CUCUMBERS	After all danger of frost; sow again 4–5 weeks later	Seeds ½" deep; thin to 12" apart in rows 4'–6' apart
PEPPERS	Sow indoors 8–10 weeks before last spring frost; set out plants after all danger of frost	Plant outdoors 18"–24" apart in rows 2'–3' apart
SUMMER SQUASH (including Zucchini)	After all danger of spring frost	Seeds 1" deep; thin to 18" apart in rows 3'–4' apart
SWISS CHARD	Mid to late spring	Seeds ½" deep; thin to 6"–10" apart in rows 18" apart
TOMATOES	Sow indoors 6 weeks before last spring frost; set out plants after all danger of frost	Plant outdoors 18"–30" apart in rows 3'–4' apart; Grow in wire cages or tie to stakes

Other vegetables often grown as an early summer garden crop: beets, kale, kohlrabi, okra, onions. Consult your Burpee Gardens catalog for an up-to-date listing of the best varieties for home gardens and for additional planting information.

APPROXIMATE YIELD PER 10' ROW	APPROXIMATE DAYS TO HARVEST	NOTES
12 lbs.	49–60	Bush beans mature faster than pole beans but have shorter picking season.
15 lbs.	60–65	More productive than bush beans over longer season. Some people prefer the richer flavor.
10 lbs.	65–76	Plant Little Finger or Short 'n Sweet for "baby" carrots; Toudo Hybrid and other Nantes types have best flavor.
12–15 ears	63–92	Some newer varieties should not be sown until soil is thoroughly warm; some varieties need isolation from other varieties for best flavor. See catalog or seed packets.
12 lbs.	55–70	"Burpless" varieties are easier to digest; grow on trellis or fence for straight fruits. For small garden, try short-vine bush types.
6 lbs.	57–80 *	Sweet and hot peppers are grown the same way. For beautiful salads and relish trays, grow several varieties of sweet peppers maturing to yellow, red, and purple
15 lbs.	50–57	Grow a few plants of several different types: yellow and green zucchini; white or yellow Patty Pan; yellow straight neck or crook-neck. Squash is incredibly productive if kept picked.
7–10 lbs.	50–60	The almost fail-proof vegetable; spring planting can be picked as needed all summer and fall.
30–60 lbs.	52–80 *	Pixie Hybrid bears the earliest fruits; Supersteak Hybrid or Delicious the largest; Roma VF is best for sauce, canning; Burpee's Long-Keeper stays fresh at room temperature for several months. Grow several varieties until you find the flavors you like best.

From time plants are set out in garden to time of first harvest

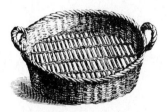

A · B · O · U · T · T · H · E · A · U · T · H · O · R

Austrian-born Perla Meyers grew up in Barcelona, Spain, with her Viennese mother and Alsatian father. She graduated from the University of Interpreters School and worked for the United Nations in major European cities. In Geneva, she became interested in cooking and food and began intensified study with École Hotelière, the Cordon Blue School, and the Hotel Sacher.

She began her own cooking school in New York in 1960, and now lectures and teaches students how to shop properly and prepare food with a creative attitude. Besides writing best-selling books, appearing on radio and television, and teaching, Ms. Meyers travels throughout Europe visiting markets and working in great restaurants. She lives with her husband and son in New York City and Connecticut.